To Mila

MANAGEMENT ACCOUNTING IN PRACTICE

MANAGEMENT ACCOUNTING IN PRACTICE

by

F. A. CALLABY

F.C.C.A., F.C.M.A., F.C.I.S.

GEE & CO (PUBLISHERS) LIMITED

151 STRAND, LONDON WC2R 1JJ

1972

FIRST PUBLISHED 1972

Previously published under title *Illustrations of Management Accounts in Practice*, 1959

© Gee & Co (Publishers) Limited
SBN 85258 109 2

A/658. 1'5/1

Made and Printed in Great Britain by
GEE & CO (PUBLISHERS) LIMITED, LONDON AND ST ALBANS

CONTENTS

PREFACE

So many books have been written about management accounting during the past few years, that one approaches with doubt the responsibility of presenting another.

However, there remains a need for a practical work on the subject, which will nevertheless make the principles of management accounting quite clear. It is believed that this book should help the student and the accountant in both aspects.

That accounting is an aid to management has been known for centuries, else why should management have used it, but during the earlier part of this century the demands of the Companies Act, the City of London and the Inland Revenue had tended to encourage the development of the financial aspects of accounting and the audit and check functions.

The First World War showed the need for cost control in industry and from this need was born The Institute of Cost and Management Accountants.

The Second World War reinforced the demand for cost control and the Americans under the Marshall Plan gave the next impetus.

A British team of accountants representing five accountancy bodies and a number of managers were sent to America in 1950 to investigate methods of accounting control and its contribution to the high industrial productivity achieved in the U.S.A.

This team produced a best-selling report entitled 'Management Accounting'.

And so the name was conceived, and with it a concept of the accountant working for and in conjunction with management, with the purpose of establishing planning and control over current and future operations.

Since that time management accounting has taken a new dimension, having been linked with the behavioural sciences recognizing that any technique involving planning and control must involve itself with human objectives and human resources.

It was my privilege to be one of the management accounting team and it was in 1953 that I made an address entitled 'Accounting for Human Nature', which was afterwards re-printed in the United Kingdom and in the United States.

This was the first impetus towards appreciating the human aspects of accounting work.

At this moment, I would like to pay tribute to Mr Ian T. Morrow, C.A., F.C.M.A., as leader of the management accounting team.

To many he is known as a 'business doctor'. To me he will always be the midwife of management accounting.

As this work is an up-dating of a successful book entitled *Illustrations of Management Accounts in Practice*, I must give my full acknowledgement to Sir Anthony Burney, O.B.E., B.A., F.C.A., for the illustrations and other matter which have been used in the new edition.

Darlington   F. A. CALLABY.
1972.

Chapter I

THE ROLE OF MANAGEMENT ACCOUNTING

It is most desirable before proceeding further to make sure that we know what is meant by the term management accounting.

Like most concepts that have become fashionable, the outlines have become a little blurred, so let us get to first principles.

The management accounting team in the Anglo-American Productivity Report in 1950 gave the following definition:

'Management accountancy is the presentation of accounting information in such a way as to assist management in the creation of policy, and in the day-to-day operation of an undertaking.'

A study group, set up by The Association of Certified Accountants defined management accounting as follows:

'The application of accounting and statistical techniques to the specific purpose of producing and interpreting information designed to assist management in its functions of promoting maximum efficiency and in envisaging, formulating, and co-ordinating future plans and subsequently in measuring their execution.'

I think the latter definition the better because it emphasizes that the information is 'selected' and that the management activity is that of planning and co-ordinating. By this the whole concept is enlarged.

No matter what techniques of accounting, statistics and mathematics are used, no matter what mechanical aids are adopted, computer or otherwise, these techniques do not in themselves constitute management accounting.

In the rapidly developing world of computers, the applications of these devices to the supply of information to management has been termed 'informatics'. Too much has been claimed for this, for while it may give speedy information, substantial analysis of information, and economies in obtaining information, it remains yet just one more technique.

It is in the manner of selection, form of presentation and above all in the use of information selected that determines whether the adjective management can truly be applied.

During recent years the behavioural sciences have made considerable inroads into business management thought, and in the fields of management training and education it is now realized that there is a vast difference between the acquiring of techniques and their application in the actual spheres of human activity.

Skill and special ability is required to apply these techniques into the management process which begins and ends with the management of men.

This position applies equally to accounting. Historical accounting, product costing and annual accounts may each serve a very useful purpose but may have little effect upon management action or in providing dynamism to an organization.

It was Mr T. G. Rose, famous for his concept of higher control in management, who said 'he could feel the urgency in a company operating under budgetary control'.

A recent inquiry into a number of successful businesses for the reasons for their success, showed great variation in their methods and philosophies of management but that the common factor apparently contributing to success was a close and exact financial control.

There are available many methods of accounting; budgetary control, costing, statistical and mathematical techniques. It is in the selection of these techniques, in the choice of information to be supplied and recognition of the human needs of the organization that shows the skill, experience and insight of the management accountant.

Much is written today concerning the importance of communication in the conduct of business affairs. Management accounting is a very important part of the communication system of any company or organization where financial control is necessary.

Basically information leads to action. Correct and appropriate information permits planning and guidance, comparative figures provide a sense of urgency to action or competition, and departmental reports provide a basis for decentralization and control schemes such as management by objectives.

Therefore the management accounting system must be tailored to provide information for action, timed for maximum impact, direct and simple for immediate comprehension and co-ordinated for planning and control.

CHAPTER II

MANAGEMENT ACCOUNTING *v.*
FINANCIAL ACCOUNTING

This book is addressed to all classes of accountants and in doing this recognizes the two main streams of accounting activity – the practising and the industrial/commercial.

In the United Kingdom, accountants may train through the practising accountant's office and qualify through an Institute of Chartered Accountants or The Association of Certified Accountants. They may otherwise obtain their training and experience through industrial works or commercial office and qualify through The Association of Certified Accountants or The Institute of Cost and Management Accountants.

The different channels of training and experience result in accountants with somewhat different outlooks.

Accountants who develop within an industrial/commercial milieu think in terms of costs, control, planning, profitability and management reports. Accountants trained and operating within a professional accountant's office, think more in terms of audit procedures, security, compliance with company law and statutory regulations, the interests of shareholders and the responsibility for an audit report.

Both classes of accountant are an essential element in the business life of the nation although the older historically and probably the most conservative aspect of the practising accountant has tended to be overshadowed in recent years by the emergence of the management accountant who not only uses the specialized systems of costing, accounting, marginal costing, standard costing, and budgeting control, but also such techniques as statistical control, operational research, discounted cash flow, computer 'informatics' and operational audits.

The medium and larger businesses can usually employ qualified and experienced accountants as management accountants, but it must not be overlooked that the bulk of the small business owners rely upon their auditors to guide them in all matters relating to finance, accounting and taxation.

This situation has been accepted by the larger accountancy

firms who have set up consultancy departments or associate firms specializing in the industrial aspects of accountancy.

In the smaller firms of professional accountants it may be necessary for one partner to make himself familiar with management accounting techniques and to strengthen the staff with men suitably qualified in the industrial field.

There are obvious difficulties in installing specialist staff among general practitioners, but there is little doubt that properly carried out it can be profitable for the professional firm and what is probably more important will add materially to the service that accountancy firms can offer their clients.

In approaching management accounting, the general practitioner may often need to rid himself of certain intellectual attachments such as the belief that making 'improvements' to financial accounts can be a substitute for properly planned management accounts as illustrated within these pages.

There are essential differences between the financial accounts prepared for shareholders and the public and those accounts prepared to establish control of a business and to act as a guide and spur to management.

The main differences between financial and management accounts lies in the differences in the focus of control.

In financial accounts figures are collected under the heading of expense irrespective of what purpose the expense is put to, although it may broadly differentiate between manufacturing, trading, and profit and loss headings.

In management accounting, the information is analysed to function, and to department or cost centre so that expenditure or receipts can be controlled under the concept of 'accounting for responsibility'.

This method of information analysis involves the preparation of complex accounting codes the importance of which increases with the introduction of office mechanization, especially when punched cards and computerized controls are introduced.

Furthermore, the time elements in the preparation and presenting of each type of accounting information is strikingly different.

In the case of financial accounts it is customary to prepare the accounts once a year.

This is quite unacceptable by management accounting standards. The preparation of budgets and business plan may be an annual event, but the reports on progress and activity differ according to the needs of the situation.

Some types of business find quarterly accounting returns sufficient for control purposes, but in the main, accounting periods of one calendar month or artificial 'months' of four weeks and five weeks are used.

Information for control of activities on the shop floor may be required weekly and it is not unknown for such information to be needed daily in certain fast moving operations.

The frequency of accounting returns is dependent upon the needs of the user. If figures are presented too frequently it may not be possible to see trends adequately and if too infrequent the information may be too late for effective action to be taken. Correct timing gives maximum impact and creates action. Under the stress of special circumstances the normal timing may need to be changed.

The other great difference between financial and management accounts is the use of budgeting control procedures. Although it is the practice to show last year's figures in the presentation of annual accounts, such comparison may be useless because of changes in circumstances, unsatisfactory because they involve looking backward into the past, and because of the nature of the expenses analysis the extra expenses or reduction in expenses in certain functional areas may be compensating.

The introduction of budgetary control is an important psychological act: at that moment the management moves away from a *laissez-faire* method of running the business over to a method of forward planning, measured control and accounting for responsibility.

By the use of management accounting techniques, it is possible to lay down a formal plan, co-ordinate individual or departmental plans, record progress, check divergencies, employ incentives to improve efforts in output, expense reduction or profitability.

The other important difference between the two types of accounts is in the speed of preparation.

In financial accounts the preparation is too often a leisurely affair, dependent on balancing the books, determining outstanding assets and liabilities, taking stocks and the completion of the audit.

In the preparation of management accounts, stress is placed

upon the speed of preparation. This will certainly involve approximation; it may require statistical stock control and certainly a degree of error will be 'built-in'. With an acceptable degree of 'commercial tolerance' the procedures are employed to give speed and reliability to the presentation of information to management and so provide the maximum degree of control and of action.

CHAPTER III

MANAGEMENT ACCOUNTING STATEMENTS
FOR A SMALL CONCERN

This chapter contains a description and an explanation of the management accounting statements suitable for a comparatively small engineering concern, employing about three hundred people and producing castings and mechanical and scientific instruments; the castings are made for the company's own products and also to customers' requirements. In all there are about sixty different products and, with the different sizes and types of each, their total number runs into many hundreds.

The factory is divided into two casting shops, a moulding shop, a fettling shop, a machine shop, and two assembly shops. The quality of the products is controlled by the inspection department. The service departments in the factory consist of a tool-room and drawing office, stores and dispatch department, and a maintenance department. Purchasing, progressing, wages, costing, estimating, and the works office are treated for accounting purposes as a service department called works general. In addition there are secretarial, accounting, and sales offices which, with the managing director's office, form the selling and administration department.

The new system is designed to provide a set of financial accounts once a year, and a set of management accounts in standard cost form every period of four or five weeks, within twelve working days after the end of the period.

Outline of the accounting and costing system
As the system by which these accounts are prepared is explained fully in Chapters VII and VIII, it is unnecessary to do more here than to give a brief description of it. One general ledger is kept from which both financial and management accounts are prepared. Each account in the general ledger is coded with a four-figure number. The first two digits identify the group of accounts and the second two digits the account itself. Thus, account 01.07 is the fixtures and fittings account (07) in the fixed assets group (01). Balance sheet accounts are kept in the

first section of the ledger and profit and loss accounts in the second section. The profit and loss account section is again subdivided into: (a) conventional expense and revenue accounts and (b) departmental operating accounts and variance accounts.

At the end of each accounting period all the subsidiary day-books are posted direct to the general ledger. Expenditure which is not wholly concerned with the current period is posted to a prepayments and accruals ledger, and transfers are made from this ledger to the expense accounts of the amounts actually attributable to the accounting period concerned.

The actual expenditure in the 'primary' accounts in the general ledger (purchases, wages, and expenses accounts) is then transferred at standard cost either direct, or through the departmental operating accounts, to accounts for stocks, work in progress, or to selling and administration expenses. The differences between standard and actual costs are variances and are transferred to separate accounts. The standard cost of sales is transferred from the work in progress account to the standard cost of sales account.

The balances on the general ledger accounts resulting from this re-analysis of expenditure can then be entered directly on to the statement of financial position and on to the profit and loss account in standard cost form.

This procedure, whereby the expenditure of the company is analysed under conventional expense headings before being re-allocated to departments, makes the work of the auditors quite simple and straightforward.

Such a procedure ensures that the cost accounting and financial accounting figures are identically based and avoids any necessity for integration.

Monthly statements to the board
The statements described below are presented to the board and management each month. They provide useful information on all the main aspects of the company's financial position and trading. Not only is the actual income and expenditure of the business shown for the current period and for the cumulative periods to date, but the variances from the budget are also shown; this is important, for by a study of these variances top management can effectively maintain control over the company's affairs. The information supplied in these statements is

in monetary terms. This may be supported from time to time by information in physical or quantity terms. It is, however, of primary importance for top management to know the financial progress of the business. In particular they should know how the actual results have varied from the budgets which have been approved by the board as representing their financial plans for the year.

Profit and loss account (*Exhibit No. 1*)

This statement is drawn up in standard cost form. It shows the net margin which is the profit which would have been earned on actual sales if the cost of production, selling and administration had been in accordance with standard. It then goes on to show how the actual costs vary from standard under a number of different headings, arriving finally at the actual net profit for the period before taxation.

Instead of 'net margin' some authorities would use 'standard profit' (viz. Institute of Chartered Accountants' booklet *Standard Costing*). To use 'standard profit', however, presupposes that the sales were made at standard selling prices; in Exhibit No. 1 this cannot be assumed and so the term 'net margin' has been used.

For ease of presentation, the effect on profits of the difference between actual and budgeted sales is not shown on the profit and loss account. This is shown on the statement of sales and margins (Exhibit No. 4).

It will be noted that the variances arising on overhead expenses are analysed between 'volume' and 'spending'. Further reference to this analysis is made later in this chapter. For the moment its importance may be stressed by referring to the expenses of the production departments where it will be seen that there is a gain of £1,455 due to under-spending and a loss of £1,365 resulting from an under-recovery of expenses due to a lower volume of production than budgeted. If the variances were not analysed in this way, and only the net variance of £90 was shown, the under-recovery of expenses would not be disclosed and the position would probably be considered as satisfactory; if, however, the fall in volume of production is due to a lack of customers' orders then this is far from being the case.

All the variances shown in the profit and loss account are

Exhibit No. 1

PROFIT AND LOSS ACCOUNT

	Five weeks to June 30th, 1972 Period 6			Twenty-six weeks to June 30th, 1972 Periods 1–6		
	£	£	£	£	£	£
TOTAL SALES ..			58,550			279,521
Less Works standard cost of sales ..			38,524			194,068
GROSS MARGIN ..			20,026			85,453
Less Standard cost of selling and administration ..			6,310			31,076
NET MARGIN ..			13,716			54,377
VARIANCES: Gains or *Losses**						
Price: Purchase of materials ..		278			1,201	
Production Departments Labour:						
Rates of pay	*580**			*2,272**		
Efficiency ..	289			1,157		
Materials: Usage ..	*89**			*458**		
Expenses: ..						
Volume ..	*1,365**			*7,111**		
Spending ..	1,455	*290**		*4,740**	*13,424**	
Service Departments Expenses:						
Volume ..	*2,054**			*8,738**		
Spending ..	630	*1,424**		6,893	*1,845**	
Selling and Administration Expenses:						
Volume ..	*396**			*3,796**		
Spending ..	*1,514**	*1,910**		*751**	*4,547**	
			*3,346**			*18,615**
Plus			10,370			35,762
Net proceeds from sale of scrap ..			7			3,418
			10,377			39,180
Less Miscellaneous expenditure ..			—			178
ACTUAL NET PROFIT BEFORE TAXATION			£10,377			£39,002

discussed later. The materials price variance, however, needs a brief explanation here because of its effect on the monthly profit as shown in the profit and loss account. This variance is the difference in value between the standard and actual prices of materials purchased during the period. The difference is written off to the profit and loss account regardless of whether the materials have been used or are in stock. Thus, the stock of materials is shown in the statement of financial position at standard price and not at actual cost. An adjustment is usually made at the end of the financial year revaluing the stock on the basis of cost or market prices, and in some concerns it is considered necessary to make an adjustment in the monthly management accounts. A method of calculating the adjustment is explained in Chapter VIII.

Statement of financial position (Exhibit No. 2)
This is merely a balance sheet in vertical form showing the changes in the various items during the period and since the beginning of the financial year.

It is a statement with which most accountants are familiar and does not, therefore, require any further explanation or comment. It is doubtful, however, whether it is worth while producing every month in its present form. It is true that from this statement it is possible to work out how current profits are being used in the business, and to compare the increase in fixed assets with the capital expenditure budget and the increase or decrease in the bank balance with the cash forecast. Nevertheless, it may be thought preferable to prepare a movement of funds statement showing the sources and uses of funds, and to show the actual expenditure on fixed assets and the bank balance on their respective budgets.

Statement of stocks and work in progress (Exhibit No. 3)
This statement, which is specifically prepared for the management, provides an analysis of the stocks and work in progress accounts.

Stocks of raw materials are stated at standard prices. Work in progress comprises (*a*) bought-out parts at standard prices, and (*b*) work in progress, including finished goods, at the standard cost of raw materials, labour, and works overheads. To save work in the cost department, purchases of bought-out

Exhibit No. 2

STATEMENT OF FINANCIAL POSITION

	June 30th, 1972		Increase/ Decrease* from May 26th, 1972	Increase/ Decrease* from January 1st, 1972
	£	£	£	£
FIXED ASSETS at written-down value:				
Leasehold land and buildings	8,222		20*	115*
Buildings extensions ..	25,817		78*	44*
Plant and machinery ..	45,604		1,130	2,640
Fixtures and fittings ..	3,799		126	343
Office furniture	3,075		118	99
Motor vehicles	609		15*	252*
Canteen equipment	264		2*	14*
Loose tools	96		5*	45*
Plant on hire-purchase ..	13,226		1,350*	822
		100,712	96*	3,434
CURRENT ASSETS:				
Stocks and work in progress	147,712		1,784	35,901
Trade debtors *less* provisions	90,248		8,333*	1,064
Prepayments and sundry debtors	10,695		1,998	5,712
Bank balance and cash in hand	1,577		1,070*	3,751*
	250,232		5,621*	38,926
Less CURRENT LIABILITIES:				
Trade creditors	51,384		11,838*	17,052*
Hire-purchase creditors ..	5,541		800*	1,165*
Accruals and sundry creditors	35,163		15*	6,676
Current taxation	2,833		593*	1,480*
Bank overdraft	79,822		14,686*	8,531*
	174,743		27,932*	21,552*
NET CURRENT ASSETS		75,489	22,311	60,478
SUBSIDIARY COMPANIES:				
Cost of investments ..	8,556		—	—
Less Credit balances on current account	6,424		4,838	2,090*
		2,132	4,838*	2,090
NET ASSETS		£178,333	£17,377	£66,002
NET ASSETS REPRESENTED BY:				
Ordinary shares	70,000		7,000	27,000
Capital reserves	484		—	—
Profit and loss account:				
Balance at 1.1.1972 ..	63,414		—	—
Surplus, twenty-six weeks to date, before taxation	39,002		10,377	39,002
Reserve for future taxation	5,433		—	—
		£178,333	£17,377	£66,002

Exhibit No. 3

STATEMENT OF STOCKS AND WORK IN PROGRESS

A/c. No.	Details	Amounts as at June 30th, 1972	Increase/*Decrease**from May 26th, 1972	January 1st, 1972
		£	£	£
07.01	Stocks of raw materials	13,614		
07.03	Materials unused in departments ..	1,642		
	Raw materials stock at standard prices	15,256	*923**	5,477
07.02	Work in progress, including bought-out parts and finished stocks:			
	(a) Materials and bought-out parts	60,898	2,100	21,135
	(b) Direct labour	20,404	317	2,971
	(c) Works overheads	45,559	869	6,523
	Work in progress at standard cost	126,861	3,286	30,629
07.04	Stock and work in progress reserve (difference between stocks at January 1st, 1956, valued per balance sheet and at 1956 standard prices)	*Cr. 1,239*		
07.06	Chargeable tools and dies, work in progress	322	*120**	*455**
07.07	Stocks of packing materials ..	861	40	*11**
07.08	Stocks of consumable stores ..	2,537	*194**	82
07.09	Stocks of consumable tools ..	1,270	*132**	105
07.10	Stocks of printing and stationery	1,361	*96**	38
07.11	Stocks of replacement parts for plant, machinery and equipment	483	*77**	36
		6,512	*459**	250
	Total stocks and work in progress per statement of financial position	£147,712	£1,784	£35,901

ANALYSIS OF WORK IN PROGRESS (A/c. No. 07.02)

	£	£	£
(a) Stocks of bought-out parts and work in progress in shops	101,510	2,413	25,322
(b) Stocks of finished products	25,351	873	5,307
	£126,861	£3,286	£30,629

parts are charged direct to the work in progress account instead of charging the purchases to a separate stock account, and then transferring issues from stores to the shops. For the same reason finished stocks are not evaluated and transferred from work in progress until sold.

Each month, however, the management needs an analysis between (a) the value of work in progress in the shops, and (b) the value of finished stocks unsold. A physical stocktaking of finished stocks is therefore made and evaluated at works standard cost. This is not difficult as finished stocks would be small. The value of uncompleted work in the shops is obtained by deducting the value of finished stocks from the total of the work in progress account.

From this statement the management can see how much money is tied up in stocks and work in progress, and whether the amount is reasonable in relation to the resources available and to the volume of business.

Statement of sales and margins (Exhibit No. 4)
This statement shows for each of the main product groups the actual and budgeted sales and the gross margins after deducting the works standard cost of sales. The total figures for actual sales (column 1), works standard cost on actual sales (column 3) and the gross margin (column 5) are as shown on the profit and loss account (Exhibit No. 1).

The difference between the gross margin obtained on actual sales for the period (column 5) and the gross margin on budgeted sales (column 7) is shown in column 9. From this column, therefore, can be seen which product groups have earned a gross margin in excess of the budget and which have earned a gross margin below the budget.

The variances shown in column 9 between the actual and budgeted gross margin are not analysed under the usual headings of sales price, sales volume and sales mix variances. To do this it would have been necessary to calculate the works standard cost and the cost of this clerical operation was considered excessive. Should a situation develop when the additional information becomes necessary then the extra analysis can be made.

Certain conclusions, however, can be drawn from the available figures; for example, the actual sales (£76,532) of Product

A for periods 1–6 were in excess of the budgeted sales (£72,904), but despite this increase in volume there was still an unfavourable gross margin variance of £5,347. The sales analysis showed that by and large the actual prices obtained for the products in this group were near enough to the budgeted prices and therefore the fall in the gross margin percentage from 48 per cent on budgeted sales to 38·7 per cent on actual sales was due to the mix of actual sales being less profitable than the budgeted mix to an extent which more than offset the effect of the increase in the volume of sales.

Departmental operating statement (Exhibit No. 5)

A departmental operating statement provides the foreman in each works department with a summary of the cost results of his department for the period concerned, and cumulatively for the financial year to date.

The cost of production is analysed between direct wages, materials and expenses, and the difference between standard and actual cost is further analysed under major headings.

The variances shown on Exhibit No. 5 are those which are considered necessary and practical at the outset of a scheme. In time, however, it is possible that further variances be introduced to enable the foremen to exercise more detailed control over the operating costs of their departments. It is, probably, much better to start a scheme with only those variances which are essential. The introduction, from the outset, of every possible variance – in case they should be needed – imposes an unnecessary burden on both staff and management at a time when this is best avoided.

The price variance on materials does not appear in this statement as it is transferred to the profit and loss account at the purchase accounting stage and materials are therefore dealt with in the accounts at standard cost, anyhow such variances are not the concern of the foreman.

The expenses and the analysis of the total variance between volume and spending are considered in detail in the next section.

Works department – schedule of expenses (Exhibit No. 6)

The expenses of each department are broken down in further detail and Exhibit No. 6 shows an analysis of the overhead expenses appearing on the departmental operating statement Exhibit No. 5).

Five weeks to
  Period 6
  Product Gr(
    A ..
    B ..
    C ..
    D ..
    E ..
    F ..

Chargeable

Total

Twenty-six we
  Periods 1–6
  Product Gr(
    A ..
    B ..
    C ..
    D ..
    E ..
    F ..

Chargeable

Total

Exhibit No. 4
facing page 16

Exhibit No. 5

DEPARTMENTAL OPERATING STATEMENT
(*Losses**)

Department: .... CASTING 'A'

Period 6
Five weeks ended June 30th, 1972

Level of activity: 80 per cent
Labour efficiency: 101 per cent

	A	B	C	D	E	F
Direct wages					**Analysis of variance**	
		Standard	Actual	Total variance	Rates of pay	Efficiency
		384	398	*14**	*19**	5
Materials		Standard	Actual	Total variance usage		
		2,980	3,130	*150**		
Expenses	Allowed	Standard	Actual	Total variance (B – C)	Analysis of variance	
					Volume (B – A)	Spending (A – C)
	1,694	1,536	1,768	*232**	*158**	*74**
Total		Standard	Actual	Total variance		
		£4,900	£5,296	£*396**		

Periods 1–6
Twenty-six weeks ended June 30th, 1972

Level of activity: 81 per cent
Labour efficiency: 107 per cent

	A	B	C	D	E	F
Direct wages					**Analysis of variance**	
		Standard	Actual	Total variance	Rates of pay	Efficiency
		2,028	1,963	65	*70**	135
Materials		Standard	Actual	Total variance usage		
		16,554	16,937	*383**		
Expenses	Allowed	Standard	Actual	Total variance (B – C)	Analysis of variance	
					Volume (B – A)	Spending (A – C)
	8,866	8,113	10,155	*2,042**	*753**	*1,289**
Total		Standard	Actual	Total variance		
		£26,695	£29,055	£*2,360**		

The items of expenses are divided into two broad groups, (*a*) those which are directly chargeable to the department and (*b*) those which are charges from service departments. These groups are subdivided into expenses controllable by the foreman and other expenses chargeable to the department. The purpose of this schedule is twofold: first to show the foreman which expenses and variances are within his direct control, and, secondly, to show him what other expenses have been included in his departmental budget and overhead rate. Although he may not have direct control over the latter expenses he is often able to exercise some measure of influence over them.

The indirect labour items, except waiting time, have been treated as falling outside the foreman's control. In certain circumstances it might be considered that indirect labour should be allocated as a charge within the direct control of the foremen. In this example, however, although the foremen are responsible for indirect labour from the point of view of shop discipline, the number and cost of indirect workers in the production departments are determined at a higher level in the organization.

Waiting time, however, is considered as being within the control of the foremen since, in normal circumstances, they organize the distribution of work within their departments.

Column 1 shows the budgeted expenses for each item for the period at 100 per cent level of activity, i.e. five weeks' proportion of the annual budgeted amount. The budgeted expenses for each department are made up of:

(*a*) fixed expenses – those expenses which are regarded as being fixed irrespective of the level of activity;

(*b*) variable expenses – those expenses which are regarded as being directly variable with the level of activity;

(*c*) semi-variable expenses – those expenses which lie between those which are fixed and those which vary directly; they vary with, but not in direct proportion to, activity. In this department semi-variable expenses have been assumed to be half fixed and half variable.

The preceding column indicates the category into which the expenses fall.

On this statement it has been assumed that fixed expenses remain fixed and that variable expenses vary directly with the volume of production. It must be realized, of course, that

DEPARTMENT.....

ITEMS

DIRECT CHARG
Controllable
Waiting tii
Electricity

Gas ..
Consumab
Consumab
Repairs – I
Scrap ..

Other items c
ment:
Indirect lal
National Ii
labour)
Salaries ai
ance ..
Holiday cr
Rent ..
Rates (Gei
Heating
Repairs to
Depreciati

CHARGES FROM
MENTS
Controllable
Maintenan
Tool-room
Other items c
ment:
Works gen
Stores and

Exhibit No. 6
facing page 18

A Guide to Methods

for Estimating Microbial Numbers

and Biomass in Fresh Water

by

J. GWYNFRYN JONES

Freshwater Biological Association

FRESHWATER BIOLOGICAL ASSOCIATION
SCIENTIFIC PUBLICATION No. 39

1979

PREFACE

Good, modern ecological research depends upon an ability to estimate the sizes of the populations being studied, and freshwater microbes are no exception to this. It has been the policy of the Association to use this series to publish guides to assist those active in freshwater research, and to base these handbooks on taxonomy or methodology that has, in many cases, been developed or refined in the Association's own laboratories. Dr Jones has been studying populations of freshwater microbes for over ten years and so is well aware of the particular problems that their estimation presents. He has written a practical guide to most of the methods available which we hope will prove useful to many of those microbiologists who work with freshwater organisms. This guide pays particular attention to methods that are not well-described elsewhere. It should enable any microbiologist who has access to a small library of standard microbiological literature to embark on quantitative research in freshwater microbial ecology.

THE FERRY HOUSE
August 1979

E. D. LE CREN
Director

ISBN 0 900386 37 1
ISSN 0367-1887

1. INTRODUCTION

This book is intended for microbiologists who wish to count or determine the biomass of microorganisms in samples of freshwater origin. This aim may appear to be limited, particularly since a basic understanding of micro-biological technique (e.g. aseptic technique) is assumed, and since it is *not* intended that this should be used as a cook-book, with a recipe to be followed slavishly for each occasion. It is, hopefully, a useful collection of information which makes the reader think twice about the nature of a problem before a particular method is chosen to solve it. The information has been gleaned from conversations with colleagues as well as from considerable use of the Association's excellent library facilities. This book is, therefore, a mixture. It includes details of methods which have not been discussed in depth in the literature, while providing references and discussion of those which have recently been reviewed in other texts. In this way it is hoped that the reader will obtain enough information to solve many of the methodological problems which are encountered but often given little space in present-day papers. The product is therefore uneven in its coverage but, judging from the number and nature of inquiries received at this laboratory, there is some hope that it may satisfy a real and growing demand.

The reader may have gathered from the first paragraph of this introduction that, in an attempt to avoid unnecessary and expensive repetition of information available elsewhere, some sections of this book are relatively short. These outline the principle of the technique, but much of the discussion may be in the form of references to the literature. References marked with an asterisk in section 9 are general works on methods in microbiology and microbial ecology, and may not be referred to in this text. The reader should turn to these for further details of methodology.

Reliable quantitative estimates of numbers and biomass (which are frequently, but not always, related) are basic requirements for many research programmes, but rarely are they achieved. The ideal counting method would allow the microbiologist to count the organisms present and estimate the proportion which is viable and metabolically active. Only very rarely is this possible and usually some compromise must be accepted. Many direct count methods which are used to obtain a 'total count' do not allow the researcher to distinguish between the viable and non-viable microbe (this is particularly true of bacteria). Similarly the so called 'viable

count' techniques, which usually rely on production of visible growth of the organisms, often fail because the method used does not provide conditions under which every viable organism in the population can grow and divide. In the meantime it may be necessary to accept figures which are of largely comparative value, but these, when combined with details of other variables (e.g. biomass estimates), may provide a realistic assessement of changes which occur in the field.

The terms *quantitative* and *comparative* have appeared already and it is hoped that further reading will provide a better understanding of their meaning. *Quantitative* data provide an accurate estimate, with a stated precision, of the population size in the sample, whereas *comparative* values may tell us whether one sample contains more or fewer organisms than another, and may provide some information on the magnitude of the difference, though the actual values may not provide estimates of population means (e.g. standing crops). Thus the terms themselves provide no difficulties, but it is clear from the literature that the limitations of some methods are not fully understood. When in doubt it is advisable to conduct an independent assessment of the efficiency of a given method by testing for the recovery of added internal standards. This may be a relatively simple matter if the standard is a particular chemical or species of microbe, but where general values (e.g. the 'total' bacterial population in a water sample) are concerned, internal standards simply do not exist, because the sample contains mixed 'cultures' of live and dead organisms as well as detrital particles in the same size range. In other words, the smaller and better defined the group under investigation (the ultimate being reduction to an autecological study) the better are the chances of obtaining reliable quantitative data.

This book does not include more sophisticated methods for the measurement of metabolic activity, which often provide valuable basic or additional information. This is not to minimize the importance of such techniques, but it was felt that they would not receive adequate treatment in a volume of this size. Nor is the book sufficiently detailed to provide information on the isolation and enumeration of particular species, concerning itself with general methods for bacteria, algae, fungi and protozoa. The omission of the more sophisticated techniques required for viruses is due to the author's lack of practical experience and the paucity of reliable quantitative information in the literature.

Sampling techniques are omitted, partly because the literature abounds with descriptions of sampling apparatus (e.g. Collins et al. 1973). We also know very little about obtaining reliable quantitative information on the micro- or macrostructure of microbial communities. This would appear, therefore, to be an inappropriate point at which to make unequivocal

recommendations on sampling methodology. A summary of sampling methods used generally at this laboratory is provided by Mackereth, Heron & Talling (1978).

Statistical analysis is an integral part of any quantitative ecological study but the majority of the techniques are not unique to microbiological problems. Details of statistical analyses are therefore not provided, but merely a little guidance to the correct approach to quantitative estimates and comparison of samples. These sections are liberally sprinkled with references to the volume by Elliott (1977). This book is recommended without reservation to all who previously have delved into statistical texts and come away confused. Dr Elliott's book is concerned with samples of benthic invertebrates but, with the minimum of mental substitution, the problems discussed may be seen as ones frequently encountered by the aquatic microbiologist, e.g. those associated with small samples from an unknown parent distribution. It is not such a big step from stonefly larvae in a net to bacteria on a membrane filter. The statistical tests for techniques which are unique to microbiology (e.g. 'Most Probable Number' methods) are, however, discussed in more detail in this book. Worked examples of the application of non-parametric tests to microbiological problems are given by Jones (1973b). An appendix to the present work is provided as a summary guide to statistical methodology.

The different approaches or methods required for planktonic and benthic communities are included and an explanation of the terminology used is necessary. Those organisms living in the water, including those at the air-water interface, are here referred to as *plankton*. This is not to imply that the interface organisms, the *neuston* as they are normally called, are unimportant, but merely that the methods are intended for general use and that a specific study of the neuston is largely a sampling problem. The organisms which inhabit the sediment or solid surfaces under the water are referred to as *benthos*. Those living in or on 'soft' material (e.g. the sediment) are referred to as the *herpobenthos* and those living on solid substrata (e.g. stones, macrophytes) are the *haptobenthos*. This nomenclature follows that suggested by Hutchinson (1975) and although it may contain a subjective element it is considered preferable to a system which includes the term *periphyton* and contains many more subdivisions based on the type of surface and sediment texture.

Techniques which are often associated with the study of microbes in fresh water (e.g. methods for concentration and making permanent preparations) are also included, as are names and addresses of manufacturers. Novel and more sophisticated techniques, where they exist, are discussed at the end of relevant chapters, with adequate reference to current literature.

2. PRETREATMENT OF SAMPLES

Microbial populations in the plankton are usually so sparse that some method of concentration must be employed. Benthic samples, on the other hand, usually contain larger numbers of organisms (e.g. bacterial counts per unit volume in the surface sediment are, on average, three orders of magnitude higher than those in the water column). Here the problem is one of dilution, and of distinguishing or separating the microbes from abiological particulate material.

2.1 DILUTION OF SAMPLES

The best diluent for most purposes is a membrane-filtered aliquot of the water. For benthic material, water immediately overlying the bottom may be used. To ensure bacterial sterility of the diluent, membranes of $0 \cdot 22 \, \mu m$ pore size must be used, and if chemical or biochemical analysis of the diluted sample is to follow then polycarbonate membranes are preferred. These are chemically more inert than the cellulosic membranes (see 3.2) and consequently interfering materials do not leach out of them (this is particularly important if fluorimetric analyses are to be performed). Anoxic water must be filtered under anaerobic conditions (e.g. in a glove compartment) if changes in water chemistry and precipitation on the membrane (e.g. of ferric iron and inorganic phosphorus) are to be avoided (S. I. Heaney, personal communication). For microorganisms other than bacteria, membrane-filtered water may not be necessary, and filtration through glass fibre (particle size retention range $0 \cdot 4 – 3 \, \mu m$) or paper (particle size retention range $3–20 \, \mu m$ (quantitative grades) and $3–30 \, \mu m$ (qualitative grades)) may be adequate.

2.2 CONCENTRATION OF SAMPLES

Many plankton samples, particularly those from oligotrophic waters, are so dilute that it is impossible to observe the microbial population directly in wet mounts, or, in many instances, to measure the metabolic activity. It is therefore necessary to concentrate the sample, in such a way as not to harm

the organisms and yet with sufficient speed to ensure that the population does not change. Centrifugation is obviously a possible technique, but the sparseness of some planktonic populations is such that a considerable amount of manipulation would be required if the method were to be used routinely on a quantitative basis. It may be possible to concentrate organisms on a membrane filter if they are sufficiently robust. Quantitative removal by scraping or back-washing however is very rarely achieved. If such a method is adopted it is advisable to use polycarbonate membranes (see 3.2), which are more easily cleaned. The addition of internal standards is necessary to determine the efficiency of the recovery procedure. Organisms with structures which are chemically resistant, such as the siliceous frustule of diatoms, may be recovered by strong acid digestion of the membrane and any trapped organic matter, followed by direct examination of the residue in a counting chamber (see 4.1). Such a method provides less information than the conventional sedimentation technique (see 4.2.1) because it is impossible to assess the viability of the population after such a harsh treatment.

Although normal membrane filtration under vacuum or positive pressure is suitable only for more robust organisms, it is a variation of this technique, using very low pressures, which has probably been most successful in the gentle concentration of microbial populations. The method was originally described by Dodson & Thomas (1964) and modified slightly by Pomeroy & Johannes (1968). The apparatus, illustrated in Fig. 1, consists of two containers, one slightly smaller than the other, and usually of Perspex, although it is possible to construct quite satisfactory cheap alternatives using conventional laboratory plastic-ware such as bottles, carboys and buckets. The base of the inner container consists of a membrane or some other suitable filter, glued with an epoxy-resin or clamped into place. Sample water is transferred to the space between the containers in such a way as to maintain a head above the level of the filter. This head, usually no more than 5 cm, is sufficient to ensure gentle passage of water through the filter, a process which may be speeded by using a magnetic stirrer with the stir bar between the containers. The water which passes through the membrane is removed by suction, thus maintaining the head of sample water. The method is very effective and can be used to concentrate several litres down to a few millilitres relatively quickly. For recovery of the organisms the filter should be backwashed with some of the filtrate and rubbed gently. The speed of filtration will depend on the head of water and the area of the filter, which for sparse populations should be no less than 400 cm^2. The type and pore size of filter used will depend on whether the total population or a particular size range of organisms is of interest. A wide range of filter materials is available, including polycarbonate and

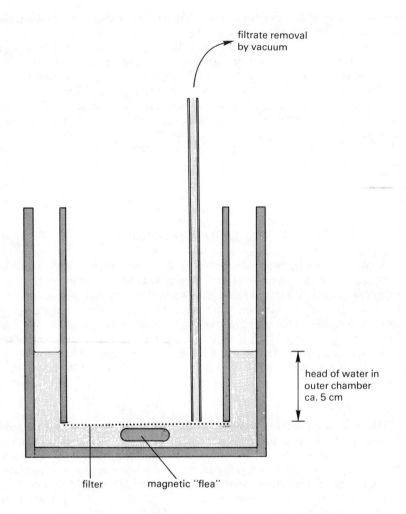

filtrate removal
by vacuum

head of water in
outer chamber
ca. 5 cm

filter   magnetic "flea"

Fig. 1   Apparatus for gentle concentration of microorganisms.

cellulosic membranes, nylon, stainless steel, nickel and copper (caution: the last two may be toxic) fine-mesh netting.   (See Appendix B).

Concentration of the sample may be advisable even if quantitative estimates of standing crop or biomass are not necessary.   There is an increasing tendency in aquatic microbiology to measure metabolic rates without reference to the populations.   Thus researchers often concentrate their efforts on the measurement of, say, respiration rate or the kinetic parameters of uptake of a particular substrate, without examining the sample to see which microorganisms are present.   It is hardly surprising that when they encounter anomalous results, they are at a loss to explain them.

2.3   HANDLING PROCEDURES

Some microorganisms are more fragile than others and handling procedures will vary accordingly.   The aim is usually to minimize the errors of handling and sub-sampling so that the value obtained is a reasonable representation of the sample.   One should therefore use the most gentle process consistent with obtaining the highest mean counts with the smallest variance, a condition which is very rarely achieved.   If biomass estimates are to be made, particularly those involving ATP analysis, then even greater care should be taken, and this is discussed in more detail in the relevant chapters.

2.3.1   *Algae*

Algae in the plankton may be mixed by gentle inversion before sub-sampling into the counting chamber.   This procedure is adequate for most forms and if counts of whole colonies are required.   Ultrasonic disruption (e.g. for up to 60 s at 12 μm) may be necessary however, to obtain reliable counts of individual cells in colonial forms such as *Microcystis* (Reynolds & Jaworski 1978).   Benthic samples are more difficult to treat satisfactorily for microscopic examination of the algae.   The herpobenthos may be gently inverted, diluted and counted in suitable chambers.   Epifluorescence examination may overcome, to a degree, the problems of seeing algae within or underneath particles, but only rarely will a complete count be obtained.   Diatoms may be counted after acid digestion of the organic material but it is necessary to have some idea of percentage viability before digestion. If direct enumeration is impossible, then some sort of separation may be necessary.   The vertical diurnal migration of certain motile forms

may be used with some success to trap them in overlying sheets of lens tissue (Eaton & Moss 1966), but if non-motile forms are to be counted it may be necessary to resort to density separation techniques. The method using colloidal silica for quantitative isolation of meiobenthos as described by Jonge & Bouwman (1977) looks particularly promising.

Problems of cell disintegration are more likely to be encountered when dealing with the haptobenthos. It has long been the convention either to remove the organisms from their substratum by scraping, or to observe the colonization of artificial substrata. However, certain diatoms, particularly *Cocconeis* spp., may disintegrate when scraped (Jones 1974), and other even more fragile forms may be encountered. If organisms must be removed from a surface then it is advisable to check by direct examination that removal is complete and that no destruction of cells has occurred. Artificial substrata may select for an artificial population and therefore direct examination of the substratum is recommended whenever possible. This may be achieved by incident light microscopy on opaque materials, e.g. the examination of diatoms on stones by epifluorescence (Jones 1974), or by transmitted light microscopy of stained sections of vegetation, etc. (Fry & Humphrey 1978). A further advantage of direct examination of solid substrata is that spatial variation (which is often considerable) may be observed and, if necessary, quantified.

2.3.2 Bacteria

These are, on the whole, more robust than algae and more rigorous techniques may be used for separation of the cells. Direct and viable counts of the bacterioplankton may be performed after shaking the sample vigorously for *c*. 30 s. Counts on membrane filters usually conform to a Poisson distribution after this treatment, as do plate counts, as long as the total number of colonies per plate is less than about 60. If this number is exceeded then a more clumped distribution may be obtained. Benthic populations may be treated in a homogenizer (e.g. 1 min in an Ultra-Turrax homogenizer) for viable counts, or by ultrasonication (30 s at 12 μm) for epifluorescence counts. Organisms which are present in the benthos as a mycelium in the vegetative stage, but produce exospores as resting stages, will show two different responses to homogenization depending on the dominant stage. Vegetative forms will exhibit a higher viable count with increasing homogenization time as the mycelium is broken into smaller viable fragments, but eventually a stage is reached where excessive disruption produces non-viable units. No such trend is seen if the organism is present predominantly in the spore form. This has been shown to be true for actinomycetes by Johnston & Cross (1976), who also demonstrated the

lethal effect of ultrasonication on vegetative hyphae. The same would probably be true for mycelia and spores of fungi if they were present in significant numbers. Ultrasonication, therefore, should not be used for viable counts, and the results with both procedures should be interpreted with care, since not only will fragmentation of some filaments occur but other more fragile forms (e.g. *Beggiatoa*) may be disrupted beyond recognition.

Haptobenthic populations should be examined directly whenever possible but particularly when quantitative estimates and spatial distribution patterns are being examined (Fry & Humphrey 1978).

2.3.3 *Fungi*

Fungi in the plankton may be treated in much the same way as bacteria. If direct counts of free-living or parasitic phycomycetes on algae are required, then prior concentration may be necessary, possibly in a counting chamber such as that described in section 4.2.1. Numbers in the benthos may be so sparse that direct counting becomes impracticable, particularly since it would not be feasible to dilute the sample to reduce the masking effect of detritus. Much of the information on fungi in fresh water has been derived from baiting and viable count techniques. The findings of Johnston & Cross (1976) with actinomycetes should be considered if it is necessary to distinguish whether the count was derived from a vegetative cell or a spore.

2.3.4 *Protozoa*

Protozoa are usually far more fragile than the other microbial groups and particular care must be taken in handling the samples. It may be necessary to prevent exposure to light, as this is often sufficient to cause lysis of sensitive benthic species. Only the minimum of sample manipulation should be used and conditions of the environment (e.g. anaerobiosis) should be maintained where possible. If dilution is necessary then gentle inversion may be used to mix the sample, and if samples are to be concentrated then the effect of fixatives and treatment should be checked for each species.

2.4 PERMANENT PREPARATIONS AND PRESERVATION OF MICROORGANISMS

The aim of a permanent preparation is the preservation of the salient features of the organism without distortion, while maintaining the original dimensions of the cell. Comparisons with fresh material should be made before any preservatives, stains etc. are used regularly. In all cases

buffered glutaraldehyde should be used if electron microscopy is needed at a later stage.

2.4.1 *Algae*

Algae may be treated in a similar way to bacteria (see 2.4.2.), if the species are able to survive membrane filtration. More fragile species are better kept in a preservative; Lugol's solution (10 g I_2, 20 g KI, 200 ml distilled H_2O; add 20 g glacial acetic acid a few days before use; store in the dark) is satisfactory for most forms, although the addition of 0·2 ml of each of 5% Tween 80, 40% formaldehyde and 20% $CuSO_4$ per 100 ml of sample may be necessary for others. Where possible samples should be kept in both preservatives. Diatoms, or at least their siliceous frustules, lend themselves more readily to preservation in a proprietary mountant after the organic matter has been removed with strong mineral acid, and the samples washed clean and dried. Live material should be examined to determine the viability of the species to be preserved, and where possible it should be retained; with care, many species can be kept alive for months.

2.4.2 *Bacteria*

Bacteria may be heat-fixed where possible and stained on glass slides. When more fragile organisms are present, suspensions may be preserved with formaldehyde, glutaraldehyde or the formalin-Tween-$CuSO_4$ mixture described for algae. Formalin-fixed samples may also be membrane-filtered and the dried membrane cleared and placed in a proprietary mountant. The method of Dozier & Richerson (1975) is convenient and suitable for a number of organisms. The dry membrane is placed on a drop of 25% glutaraldehyde (electron microscopy grade) on a slide. A second drop is spread over the membrane which is then incubated at 60 °C for 1 h. The membrane is thus cleared and fixed to the slide and may then be coated with a permanent mountant and coverslip. If other grades of glutaraldehyde are used then these should be neutralized (e.g. with solid $MgCO_3$) if fine structures such as metal encrustation on sheaths are to be preserved.

It is possible to keep dry membranes for long periods without deterioration, particularly if large bacteria with thick outer layers such as capsules or sheaths are being observed. The membranes may also be cleared in immersion oil or cedarwood oil and then stored. If, at a later date, the membranes have become cloudy they may be re-clarified by warming gently with further additions of oil. It is not possible to obtain satisfactory permanent preparations of bacteria stained with conventional fluorochromes, since any drying of the sample results in immediate reduction or loss of emission intensity.

2.4.3   Fungi

If their structures are robust enough, fungi also may be stored on membranes, but more commonly they are mounted in Amann's lactophenol (phenol 20 g; lactic acid (S.G. 1·21) 20 g; glycerol 40 g; H_2O 20 ml) sometimes with an added dye (e.g. 0·05% cotton blue or trypan blue). The preparation may be sealed with nail varnish or a suitable commercial sealing product. Details of this and alternative methods are provided by Dring (1971)

2.4.4   Protozoa

Protozoa are much more fragile than any of the above groups and only those with a hard outer 'shell' can possibly be preserved on membranes. Wet mounts may be preserved by the addition of a saturated solution of $HgCl_2$. Samples may be fixed to glass slides by the method of Nissenbaum (1953). The fixative is prepared just before use and consists of 10 volumes saturated $HgCl_2$, 2 volumes glacial acetic acid, 2 volumes formalin and 5 volumes of tertiary butyl alcohol. A drop of the suspension of protozoa is placed on a slide and then the fixative is added drop by drop until streaming stops. The slide is flooded with the fixative and left for 15 s. It is then drained and rinsed for 4 min in each of 70% iodine-ethanol and 70% ethanol. The material may then be stained and mounted in DPX mountant (BDH Ltd). Curds (1969) provides details of a more complicated procedure which produces permanent preparations of ciliates, demonstrating many fine details such as the ciliary meridians.

3. DIRECT COUNTS ON MEMBRANE FILTERS

3.1 SUMMARY OF THE METHOD

Samples of plankton or benthos, or dilutions of the latter, are drawn through membranes of given pore size which are then cleared and examined by transmitted-light microscopy, or inspected directly by incident-light illumination.

3.2 THE MEMBRANES

It is assumed that plain membranes will be used in counting all but the largest microorganisms. Grid markings affect the filtration properties of the membrane and therefore the distribution pattern of the organisms. This is true even of viable counts of bacterial micro-colonies. (Niemelä 1965).

Membranes are usually supplied as discs (diameters 10 mm to 293 mm) or as uncut sheets, with nominal pore sizes which range from $0.025\,\mu$m to $14\,\mu$m.

There are two basic types: cellulosic membranes and polycarbonate membranes.

3.2.1 Cellulosic membranes

These are made of cellulose acetate, nitrate or mixed esters of cellulose, although it is also possible to buy them of pure cellulose, nylon, PVC, Teflon or other synthetic polymers. The discs are usually $100\text{-}200\,\mu$m in depth and their structure resembles a spongy porous matrix. This depth and structure may result in an effective pore size which is somewhat smaller than the nominal size, due to adsorption of small particles within the matrix. Surface deposition of larger particles during filtration of large volumes may also contribute to blockage of the membrane. Several such membranes are manufactured (see Appendix B).

Cellulosic membranes differ widely in their characteristics and it is up to the individual to determine the most suitable product for a particular task. It is becoming apparent that direct counts (Jones & Simon 1975) and viable counts, particularly of coliforms (Geldreich 1975) may vary considerably with the type of membrane used. To date, many direct counts of bacteria have been performed on cellulosic membranes of $0 \cdot 45 \, \mu m$ pore size, particularly by epifluorescence procedures. This can cause serious underestimates, particularly if the sample contains many small bacteria, significant numbers of which may penetrate as deep as $40\text{-}100 \, \mu m$ into the body of the membrane; a few will pass through with the filtrate. Direct counts on cleared membranes may then be difficult because the organisms will be in different focal planes. In epifluorescence procedures this penetration results in low counts, because only those bacteria on or close to the membrane surface will fluoresce. Tests suggest, however, that aquatic bacteria rarely penetrate membranes of $0 \cdot 22 \, \mu m$ pore size to depths greater than $10 \, \mu m$; these are therefore more suitable for transmitted-light and epifluorescence microscopy.

3.2.2 *Polycarbonate membranes*

These are much thinner than cellulosic membranes and consist of polycarbonate sheeting (about $10 \, \mu m$ thick) which has been bombarded with high energy nuclei whose tracks are then dissolved, leaving pores of known size. The surface area available for adsorption, and the pore density, are much less than on comparable cellulosic membranes. The latter feature would normally cause much lower filtration rates but the thinness of the membrane and the decreased tortuosity of the flow-path tend to offset this to some degree. In spite of manufacturers' claims of equivalent flow rates, in our experience filtration is consistently slower with polycarbonate membranes. Size fractionation of microbial populations is however much more precise and the membrane's greater strength allows more rigorous back-washing. The membranes also possess a flat surface (one side is shiny) which is ideal for studies by scanning electron microscope. Their high static charge may sometimes cause inconvenience in handling.

3.2.3 *Black membranes for epifluorescence microscopy*

Until recently, black membrane filters were only available in pore sizes $\geqslant 0 \cdot 45 \, \mu m$, but now $0 \cdot 22 \, \mu m$ pore-size membranes are made commercially (Sartorius Ltd). These membranes are cellulosic and produce a very dark background for epifluorescence examination. Our most satisfactory results, however, have been obtained with plain white membranes we had dyed ourselves (Jones & Simon 1975). The procedure is simple and may

be applied to cellulosic as well as to polycarbonate membranes. Dye (0·25 g Dylon® No. 8, Ebony Black) and 0·25 g NaCl are dissolved in 100 ml of recently-boiled distilled water at c. 90-95 °C and filtered, while hot, through a GF/F (Whatman) glass fibre filter and then a 0·45 μm (Millipore) black membrane filter. The filtrate is then allowed to cool to room temperature. Membranes are dyed by immersion for 5 min in the filtrate after it has been warmed to 60-70 °C. This is followed by a rinse in distilled water. The membranes are placed on filter paper to absorb some moisture and then dried over silica gel at room temperature under vacuum. Hobbie, Daley & Jasper (1977) claimed significant improvements in epifluorescence counts using polycarbonate membranes (0·2 μm pore size) dyed with Irgalan black (acid black 107). Unfortunately they compared the results on these polycarbonate membranes with those obtained with 0·45 μm pore-size cellulosic filters. We have tested comparable cellulosic (0·22 μm pore size) and polycarbonate membranes (0·2 μm pore size) dyed with Dylon and Irgalan black and shown that the epifluorescence counts do not differ significantly. The main differences between the membranes are that (a) cellulosic membranes have a slightly rougher surface but provide good fluorescence contrast (b) polycarbonate membranes have a flatter surface and therefore it is possible to work in a single plane. Although the quality of polycarbonate membranes has improved recently, they may still have hydrophobic patches which must be pretreated with detergent (Hobbie, Daley & Jasper 1977); this may increase background fluorescence to a level which is distracting. Use of an ethanolic solution of a black dye, e.g. Sudan black B, (Zimmermann, Iturriaga & Becker-Birck 1978) may overcome this problem. If, for some reason, membranes of variable or unknown filtration area must be used then quantitative estimates can be obtained by making proportional counts using internal standards of micro-particles or distinctive microbes (for calculations see section 4.4).

3.2.4 *Electron microscopy*

Cellulosic membranes may be dissolved in acetone and the trapped material transferred to filmed specimen grids for examination by transmission electron microscopy (Harris et al. 1972). This is difficult to do without disturbing the sample. If, however, a scanning electron microscope is available then the bacteria may be observed, counted and their cell volumes estimated directly on the shiny surface of polycarbonate membranes. It is beyond the scope of this book to include details of the methodology which is given by Paerl & Shimp (1973). Overbeck (1974) provides an example of the application of the technique to fresh waters, and

more recently Bowden (1977) has demonstrated that results do not differ significantly from those obtained by epifluorescence counts on $0 \cdot 22 \mu m$ polycarbonate membranes.

3.3   FILTRATION

3.3.1   *The apparatus*

Two types of apparatus are generally available.   The membrane may be placed on a porous supporting base (glass frit, plastic or stainless steel) clamped to a funnel which is then attached to a Buchner flask (Fig. 2a).   The water sample above is drawn through the membrane by vacuum.   Pressure as well as vacuum filtration is possible with the alternative device – the filter holder – which usually consists of two discs, screwed together, between which the membrane is supported by plastic screens. (Fig. 2b).   The holder has luer fittings and is particularly convenient for use with syringes.   Although several holders are available, we find that the one made for polycarbonate membranes and manufactured under the trade name Swin-Lok® is particularly useful, since the design incorporates a locking plate which prevents twisting and possible tearing of the membrane.   The effective filtration area is usually larger in such holders that in the funnel type, and they are, of course, ideal for back-washing.   The major problem for quantitative studies is associated with the dead volume of liquid trapped in the holder.

3.3.2   *The procedure*

Apart from the problems of cell breakage, lysis and penetration into the membrane, and the even dispersal of clumps, particularly in benthic material, there are other difficulties in making quantitative estimates on membranes.

A major problem, that of ensuring an even distribution of organisms on the membrane, is more frequently encountered with the funnel apparatus than with the disc filter holders.   If the volume filtered is too small in relation to the size of membrane used, then the shape of the water-sample meniscus may be important, i.e. more water may be filtered through the periphery of the membrane than through the centre.   Examples of the effect of volume on the distribution pattern of bacteria were shown by Jones & Simon (1975), who concluded that for a 25-mm membrane at least 6 ml of sample should be filtered to overcome this.   This volume need not be composed entirely of water sample; indeed, this would be undesirable if large numbers of microbes were present.   If a small sample is used the volume

Fig. 2a   Membrane filter funnel assembly.

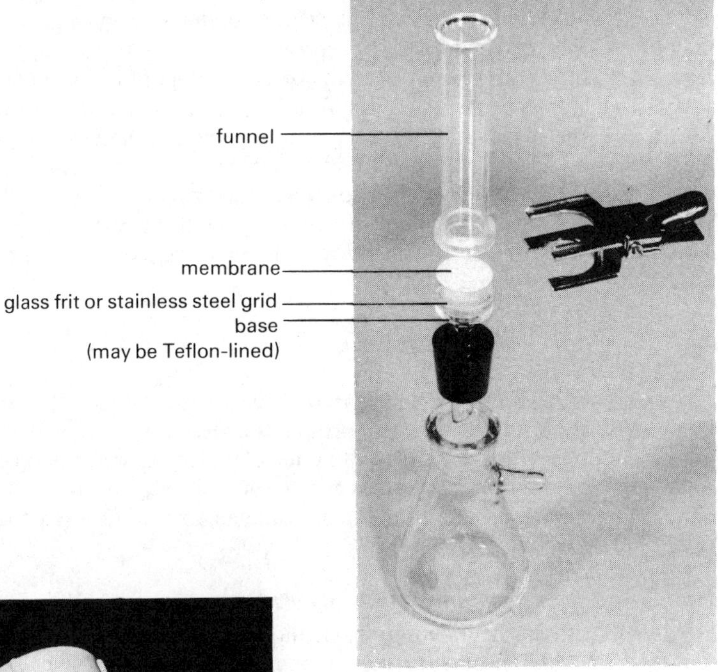

funnel

membrane

glass frit or stainless steel grid

base
(may be Teflon-lined)

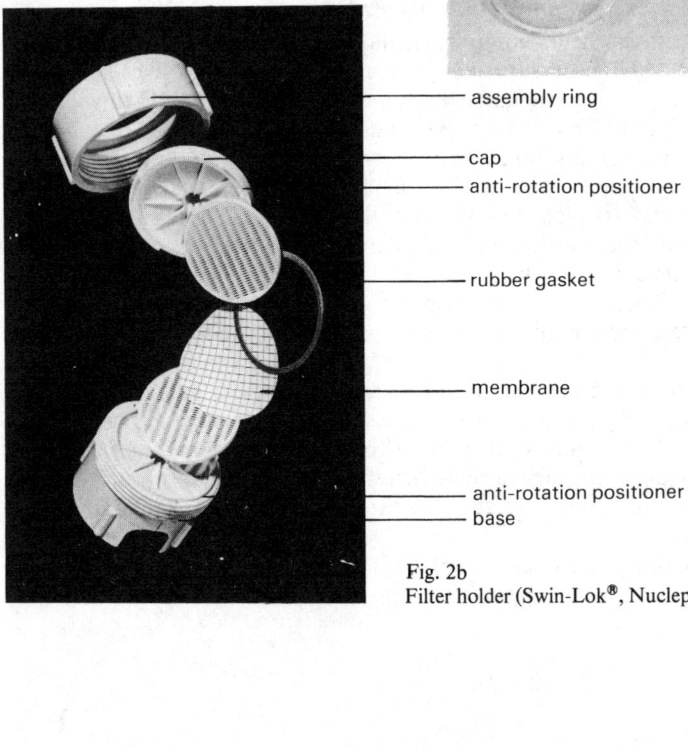

assembly ring

cap
anti-rotation positioner

rubber gasket

membrane

anti-rotation positioner
base

Fig. 2b
Filter holder (Swin-Lok®, Nuclepore Corporation).

may be made up with particle-free, or at least organism-free, water. Distilled water or sample water, prefiltered through a $0·22$-μm membrane, may be used for this purpose. Results obtained suggest that at least 3 ml should be filtered per cm^2 of membrane filtration area. These suggestions apply to the use of the funnel filtration apparatus for counts of bacteria. The distribution is more even if filter disc holders are used, but these leave a dead volume of fluid which may not evacuate completely without disturbance of the organisms on the membrane surface. This dead volume will vary with the apparatus used but with the Swin-Lok® version it is approximately $3·3$ ml for the 47-mm diameter version and $0·7$ ml for the 25-mm model.

3.4 MICROSCOPY AND ENUMERATION

The methods may be divided into three broad categories. In each a known volume of water is drawn through the membrane and a given portion of the effective filtration area is examined under the microscope and the organisms counted. For very accurate work it is advisable to check for changes in shape and size of the membrane as a result of any pretreatment used.

3.4.1 *Examination of the unstained membrane*

After filtration the membrane is allowed to dry (preferably at room temperature and, if necessary, over a mild desiccant such as silica gel). The application of heat, particularly of temperatures above 60 °C to speed the drying process, may cause curling of the membranes. The sample may be fixed before or after filtration with 2% formaldehyde. The dry membrane is then placed on a drop of immersion oil or cedarwood oil, and a second drop and a cover slip are placed on it. The fluid enters the pores and clears the membrane so that transmitted light microscopy is possible. If immersion oil is used, the cover slip may be omitted when an oil immersion objective is used. The membranes may also be cleared with glutaraldehyde; the method is described in more detail in the section on permanent preparations (see 2.3).

The methods described above are applicable only to cellulosic membranes. Polycarbonate membranes are semi-transparent, but not to a degree sufficient to allow critical microscopy. It is claimed that they may be cleared with chloroform or methylene chloride but these solvents dissolve or distort the membranes to such an extent that the spatial integrity of the filtered area is lost.

The membrane may be examined under bright-field illumination for counts of algae or larger microorganisms possessing a rigid structure such as

rotifers and morphologically distinct bacteria, e.g. ensheathed or encapsulated iron bacteria (Jones 1977). It has been suggested that total counts of unstained bacteria might be performed on such membranes (Saunders 1972) by phase-contrast microscopy. I have never had any success with this method, being unable to distinguish small bacteria from bacteria-sized particles, but it is quite suitable for larger planktonic bacteria. The phase-contrast image of material on cleared membranes is more satisfactorily resolved with a Zernicke condenser than with a Heine condenser.

3.4.2   *Examination of material stained with erythrosine*

Various staining procedures have been reported, including the use of acid fuchsin and if necessary the application of a methylene blue counterstain to the membrane itself, but erythrosine appears to be the stain most frequently used (Jannasch 1958; Razumov 1947). The dried membrane (sometimes a moist membrane may be used) is placed on a pad soaked in a 5% solution of erythrosine in 5% phenol and allowed to take up stain for a period of 1-24 h depending on the membrane and the material to be examined. The material on the membrane may be fixed in formaldehyde before staining if necessary. The membrane is then decolorized by placing it on a pad soaked in distilled water; this is repeated until the membrane is pale pink. The dried filter is cleared as above and examined under high-power magnification. Bright-field microscopy is preferred since phase contrast illumination obscures the colours obtained. The bacteria should be stained deep pink on a pale pink to colourless background. Although the method works well for large bacteria, I have encountered problems when examining samples which contained many small bacteria or significant quantities of detritus.

3.4.3   *Incident light fluorescent (epifluorescence) methods*

Fluorochromes, coupled to particular cell components, fluoresce when excited with light of a suitable wavelength. The cells are then filtered on to a black membrane and the exciting light is deflected by a dichroic mirror down through the objective on to the membrane surface. The light from fluorescing particles is of lower energy (longer wavelength) than that used for excitation and passes back up the objective and through the dichroic mirror to the eyepieces. Filters which absorb light (glass filters) or reflect it (interference filters) are chosen to provide suitable light for excitation and to select that part of the emitted light required for observation. The intensity of the image obtained by epifluorescence will depend on the light source for excitation, the light filters, the optical characteristics of the microscope, the

type of membrane filter and the type of fluorochrome and its concentration. Details of how some of these factors may affect the results obtained are given by Jones (1974), Jones & Simon (1975a) and Hobbie, Daley & Jasper (1977)

Mercury and xenon burners provide light of a suitable wavelength, the latter having the advantage of a more uniform spectral energy distribution and a longer life, but the former are generally preferred because they are cheaper and have a peak of energy in the much-used blue light region. It is possible to use quartz-iodine sources for blue light excitation but these have less power than the arc lamps. For epifluorescence (but not for transmitted-light fluorescence) the brightness of the image increases with increasing numerical aperture of the objective. Some workers also prefer to work with low-power eyepieces since these allow more light to reach the eye.

The researcher may be confronted by a wide range of possible fluorochromes to stain the microbes, either before or after filtration. Some details and references to these are given in Table 1. The concentrations are given as a rough guide but the details of the techniques should be obtained from the relevant papers. The descriptions of the sites of activity of the fluorochromes should not be accepted as absolute, since many of their reactions are not fully understood. A 5-minute staining period would be adequate for all but the optical brighteners which may require longer. These fluorochromes require ultra-violet light for excitation but have the advantage that they do not necessarily kill the organism, and may be transmitted to daughter cells on division. They may therefore be useful in estimating growth rates of natural or introduced species in mixed populations.

The fluorescein diacetate (FDA) fluorescence method may, under certain circumstances, allow direct counts of viable microorganisms to be made and may be applied to a variety of organisms on filters or in chambers. The method, originally devised for fluorimetric assay of cell-membrane bound esterase, was considered to provide an indication of the integrity of the membrane and therefore the viability of the cell (Rotman & Papermaster 1966). The non-fluorescent FDA (polar) enters the cell where it is hydrolysed, releasing the non-polar fluorescein which is retained by the cell. The reaction is immediate and is seen as a green fluorescence within the cell. The method has been used successfully for yeast cells (Paton & Jones 1975), on mammalian cells (Rotman & Papermaster 1966) and a variety of eukaryotic algae (J. A. Mowat, personal communication). We have had some success with benthic cyanobacteria, but tests with bacterial cultures and mixed populations proved too variable to be reliable (Jones & Simon 1975a). The method therefore deserves further attention and hopefully

TABLE 1. FLUOROCHROMES USED FOR DIRECT COUNTS OF MICROORGANISMS.

Fluorochrome[1]	Active site	Final concentration $mg\,l^{-1}$	Method	Excitation Light	References
Acridine derivatives					
Acridine Orange CI 46005 (AO)	Nucleic acids	10	W	Blue	Strugger (1948) Hobbie, Daley & Jasper (1977)
Euchrysine – 29NX CI 46040 (E–2GNX)	Nucleic acids	10	W	Blue	Young & Smith (1964) Jones & Simon (1975a)
Protein stains					
Fluorescein isothiocyanate (FITC)	Protein	1000	M	Blue	Babuik & Paul (1970)
Magnesium – 1 – anilino – 8 – naphthalene sulphonic acid (Mg–ANS)	Protein/cytoplasm	3500	M	uv/Blue	Mayfield (1975)
Optical Brighteners					
4, 4' – diamino – 2, 2' stilbene disulphonic acid derivatives (e.g. Photine)	Cytoplasm	500	W	uv	Weaver & Zibilske (1975)
Oxacyanine compounds (e.g. Tinopal AN)	Cytoplasm	500	W	uv	Paton & Jones (1973)
Fluorigenic esters					
Fluorescein diacetate (FDA)	Esterase enzymes	100	M	Blue	Paton & Jones (1975)
3 – 0 – methyl fluorescein phosphate (3–OMFP)	Phosphatase enzymes	100	M	Blue	Pomeroy & Johannes (1968)

W indicates that fluorochrome is applied to the water/sediment before filtration.
M indicates that fluorochrome is applied to the membrane after the water/sediment has been filtered.

[1] all the fluorochromes may be applied directly to surfaces for examination of haptobenthos.

this, or a similar fluorigenic ester, will provide some useful information on the viability of cells in natural samples. The only other reported use of such an ester which has come to my attention was that of work with methyl fluorescein phosphate by Pomeroy & Johannes (1968). In this case the enzyme responsible for cleavage would be a phosphatase, but unfortunately I have found results with bacteria to be even less reproducible than those with FDA.

The method most commonly uses a stock solution of FDA in acetone (5 g l^{-1}). This is diluted in water or phosphate-buffered saline to give a final concentration of 100 mg l^{-1} whereupon it may be mixed with a cell suspension or added to cells already concentrated on a membrane filter (Paton & Jones 1975). The reaction is almost immediate, and the fluorescence may be observed by excitation with blue light at similar wavelengths to those used for acridine fluorescence. Rotman & Papermaster (1966) in their original work with this ester noted that it tended to 'flocculate' at concentrations greater than 1 mg l^{-1}. Although we have not always worked with such dilute solutions, we have always observed precipitation at concentrations as high as 100 mg l^{-1}.

The protein stains, particularly FITC, have been used more frequently on soils but there are several reports of successful application to water (Fliermans & Schmidt 1975; Baker & Farr 1977).

Details of the application of other fluorochromes may be found in the above papers but since Acridine Orange is the most commonly used for aquatic microbes, practical details for this dye only are included here. Light filters commonly used for acridine epifluorescence include the following:

for excitation:	heat filters	Calflex B1/K2, KG1
	glass filters	GG 475, K380, K420, K480 (uv cut-out)
		BG 12 (Blue light)
		BG 38 (Red suppression)
	interference filters	S470
		KP 490 (usually mounted as 2×KP490 = KP500)
	dichroic mirror	TK 510
for emission:	suppression filter	K 515
	barrier filters	K 510, K 530

The designations given for the filters are those used by E. Leitz Ltd, and the figures usually refer to the relevant wavelengths involved (in nm units). Comparable filters are readily obtained from several sources. Because the quality of light obtained varies with so many factors, and choice of

suitable image is a subjective procedure, it is advisable to experiment with several filters until that combination which provides maximum count and acceptable contrast is obtained.

Generally speaking, the blue light used to excite acridine fluorescence in bacteria will cause fluorescence in fluorescein derivatives and also autofluorescence in chlorophyll *a*. It may therefore be used for counting algae in samples to which no dye has been added, although other combinations may be more successful where secondary pigments are responsible for photon capture. The following procedure is one that we have found satisfactory for the use of acridine dyes.

1. Dye is added as a $1 g l^{-1}$ aqueous solution to the water sample, to a final concentration of 10 mg l^{-1}, for a contact time of *c*. 5 min.
2. The sample is then filtered gently through a black $0.22-\mu m$ pore-size membrane filter. The volume should be sufficient to ensure an even distribution of the organisms on the membrane. Results suggest that at least 3 ml cm^{-2} of membrane filter area should be used. If there are large numbers of organisms the same effect is achieved by dilution with membrane-filtered distilled water or sample water.
3. The moist membrane is placed immediately on a drop of immersion oil on a slide and covered with more oil.
4. The sample is counted using a graticule of suitable area (for 25–mm diameter membranes this would be in the range $0.2-2.0 \times 10^{-3}$ mm^2).

3.5 THE ORGANISMS

Even if the gentlest filtration is achieved at very low rates, fragile organisms may be damaged or broken beyond recognition, if not during filtration then during the drying process. The method is therefore unsuitable for many aquatic protozoa and some algae, and there is some evidence to suggest that not only are bacterial counts sometimes lower than might be expected on certain membranes (Jones & Simon 1975), but that some microbes lose metabolic activity very rapidly on contact with membranes (see discussions to several papers in Stevenson & Colwell 1973).

If the organisms are sufficiently robust, membrane filtration techniques may be used to enumerate organisms whose sizes range from the smallest bacteria to the larger algae. Diatoms, for example , have been counted with some success. The living cells may be disrupted but it is still possible to count frustules, though to distinguish which algae were viable in the sample it may be necessary to apply a fixative before filtration. Larger cells, however, may be unevenly distributed on the membrane surface, and greater

numbers of diatoms are often evident at the periphery of the membrane. This is true even when detergent is added to the sample as recommended by the membrane-filter manufacturers. Counts of algae, rotifers, etc., on membranes may therefore be of value for comparative studies, but considerable care must be taken if absolute values are to be obtained.

3.6   ANALYSIS OF RESULTS

The number of organisms per unit volume of sample (n) is given by the formula

$$n = \frac{\bar{Y}.A.d}{a.v}$$

where $\bar{Y}$ is the mean count per graticule area used, A is the effective filtration area of the membrane, a is the graticule area, v is the volume of sample filtered, and d is the dilution factor (if applicable). Solvents other than water may cause the membranes to swell and therefore it may be necessary to correct for an enlarged filter area.

If larger organisms are counted on a gridded membrane then the number of grid squares in the filtering area is usually provided by the membrane manufacturer.

Before confidence limits can be calculated and parametric statistical tests applied to the results, the distribution of the data must be determined (see Elliott 1977). In many instances the microbes are found to be distributed in a random manner on membranes, thus conforming to a Poisson distribution. This has several advantages for calculation of confidence limits and allows the researcher to control the level of the confidence limits by varying the total count. The total number of organisms as a single count Y may be treated as a mean of the same value. Since we are dealing with a Poisson distribution the variance (S^2) equals the mean ($\bar{Y}$) and 95% confidence limits may be obtained from

$$Y \pm t \sqrt{\frac{S^2}{n}} = Y \pm t \sqrt{\frac{\bar{Y}}{n}}$$

The statistical notation used in this text is summarized on p. 90.

In this instance the result is a single count, confidence limits for which may be obtained from the tables of Crow & Gardner (1959) or Table 40 of Pearson & Hartley (1966). If $n\bar{Y}$ is greater than 30 then the normal

approximation holds, and since $n = 1$, the values for the 95% confidence limits on a single count Y_i are approximated by

$$Y_i \pm 2\sqrt{Y_i}$$

The larger the count, the better the values agree with the published tables, and at $\bar{Y}_i = 100$, the agreement is to within $0 \cdot 3\%$.

The precision of a count is therefore directly related to the total number of organisms counted; for example, if 100 bacteria were counted, 95% confidence limits would be

$$100 \pm 2\sqrt{100} \qquad \text{i.e. } \pm 20\% \text{ of the count}$$

and if 400 bacteria were counted those limits would be

$$400 \pm 2\sqrt{400} \qquad \text{i.e. } \pm 10\% \text{ of the count.}$$

The confidence limits are therefore easily calculated and controlled, although to obtain limits much tighter than $\pm 10\%$ the laws of diminishing returns apply and very large numbers must be counted.

There is however no guarantee that a random distribution will be obtained, especially if water with a high particulate matter content, or sediment, is being examined. In such cases, pretreatment of the sample may be necessary (see 2.1) If mixing processes fail to produce a distribution pattern for which a suitable transformation may be found, it will be necessary to count large numbers of fields per sample ($n \geqslant 50$) before reliable confidence limits can be calculated (see application of the Central Limit Theorem (Elliott 1977)).

4.   THE USE OF
COUNTING CHAMBERS

The microbial populations of the plankton are usually too dilute to be counted without prior concentration. This may be done in a variety of ways, including centrifugation and the use of sedimentation chambers or devices specially designed for dilute suspensions of delicate organisms (see 2.2). Samples of benthos may be transferred directly to chambers, or may require dilution and homogenization. A number of chambers exist, both open and closed, which vary largely in depth and the volume of sample used. In all cases it is important to avoid loss of organisms during any concentration and transfer process used, and to strike a satisfactory balance between the number of organisms and the quantity of detritus in the sample. This may be particularly difficult with benthic material where smaller organisms may be hidden by the non-living component of the sample. Choice of suitable stains and microscopic technique may help but will not obviate this problem entirely. Details of the chambers are provided in standard texts (e.g. Norris & Ribbons 1969-76) and this chapter merely suggests the uses to which they may be put, and some of the errors which may arise during their use. For convenience the chambers have been divided into two groups based on the size of the microbes to be counted. The size ranges used are arbitrary but have been found to be convenient for most freshwater microorganisms.

4.1 CHAMBERS FOR SMALLER MICROORGANISMS
($0.5\,\mu$m to $10\,\mu$m)

These are usually used for bacterial counts but have been successfully applied to other small organisms.

4.1.1   *The chambers*
The most commonly used are the Fuchs-Rosenthal haemocytometer, the Petroff-Hauser chamber and the Helber chamber. All are variants on the same basic design and consist of a glass slide, one portion of which is

carefully ground down to a known depth. This section includes a ruled graticule area for counting and is usually surrounded by a deeper moat into which excess fluid may run. A drop of sample is put on the ruled area and a coverslip is then placed so that it is supported by the slide. The organisms are counted, the number per unit area calculated, and, from this figure and the depth of the chamber, the number per unit volume obtained. The organisms may be counted in the live state by phase-contrast microscopy, or stained if bright-field microscopy is necessary, for example, when the thickness of the glass slide renders it impossible to obtain a satisfactory phase image, or when the organisms are highly motile.

4.1.2　*Errors in the use of chambers*

Several errors may arise during the use of such chambers, but before discussing these, the differences between the chambers themselves are considered. The Petroff-Hauser chamber has been reported to be unreliable for populations of pure cultures of $< 10^9$ cells ml^{-1} (Mallette 1969). This figure may be higher for the mixed and detritus-laden populations found in natural waters. It is very rarely that such population densities are found in the plankton, except possibly near sewage outfalls. A Helber chamber (Fig. 3) is used in this laboratory because it is generally considered to be better for counting bacteria than haemocytometers, most of which are 100 μm deep. The Helber chamber is 20 μm deep, and each square of the Thoma ruling is 1/400 mm^2 ($\equiv 2\cdot5 \times 10^{-3}$ mm$^2 \equiv 2500\ \mu$m^2). The volume of fluid above each square is therefore 50 000 μm^3 ($\equiv 5 \times 10^{-5}\ \mu$l). It is also possible to buy a plastic ducted version of the Helber chamber (without counting graticule), within which organisms may be allowed to settle and grow while being bathed in continually changing sample water or nutrient medium (Cruickshank, Cooper & Conran 1959). The reader is referred to Mallette (1969) for further discussion on the chambers themselves.

Errors which may occur regardless of the type of chamber used include the following:

(a) The depth of the chamber when filled may vary from sample to sample, particularly if thin coverslips are used. Chambers are often supplied with thick coverslips which must be placed carefully (i.e. until Newton's rings are observed, etc.) before the nominal chamber depth is achieved. Such coverslips may sit in either a concave or convex manner over the chamber if care is not exercised, causing variability in depth. This error may be considerably greater if thinner (No. 1½) coverslips are used, either to improve resolution or to allow the use of high-power objectives with short working distances. It is necessary to measure the depth of the chamber, each time it is filled, to obtain

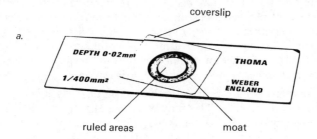

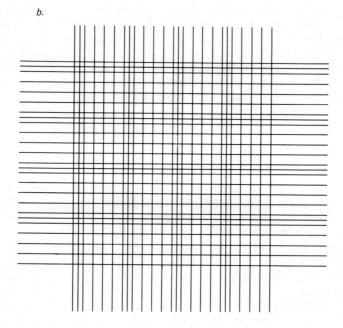

Fig. 3a Helber chamber.
   b Thoma ruling on the counting area.
      1 square = 2500 μm^2 (equivalent to a volume of 5×10^{-5} μl).

accurate results. This may be done by reading the micrometer on the fine focus control when focussing on the bottom surface of the chamber and the under-surface of the coverslip (Pike & Carrington 1972) or by aluminizing the chamber and using a microinterferometer (Norris & Powell 1961). Further information on the errors which may arise from changes in chamber depth is given by Norris & Powell (1961).

(b) Motile organisms may provide problems, particularly if they must be counted in a live state. This may sometimes be overcome by slowing them down with 0·5% (w/v) $NiSO_4$ (for smaller protozoa), or 4% polyvinyl alcohol, or methyl cellulose (for bacteria). These bacterial agents may also improve the phase-contrast image.

(c) The method of filling the chamber is important and the most reproducible results are obtained with a loop or piston pipette, placing the sample directly on the ruled area. Satisfactory distribution may still not be achieved and it may be necessary to add a small quantity of anionic detergent. When dilute samples are mixed with a magnetic stirrer, significantly higher counts are obtained at the centre of the vortex than elsewhere. Samples should be shaken, not stirred, and kept as compact as possible. If samples are allowed to spread on a surface (e.g. glass) then there will be an apparent decrease in the count, due to adsorption of the cells at the solid-liquid interface.

4.2 CHAMBERS FOR LARGER MICROORGANISMS (> 10 μm)

4.2.1 *Sedimentation chambers*

These are well known and frequently used, particularly for phyto-plankton, but, with minor modifications of technique (e.g. a change of fixative), they may be used for other large microbes, e.g. rotifers. The use of such chambers is well documented (e.g. Lund, Kipling & Le Cren 1958; Vollenweider 1974) and therefore only the minimum of detail is presented here. The chamber consists of a glass cylinder (Fig. 4a), the volume of which may be varied according to the expected density of organisms, and the base of which is suitable for observing the sedimented microbes on an inverted microscope (Utermöhl 1958). The base may be a soda-glass coverslip or disc, to which the tube of slightly smaller diameter is fixed. The end of the tube must first be ground flat. A glass solder (X76)

a.

b.

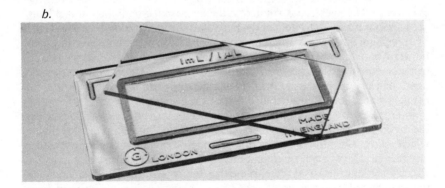

Fig. 4a   Sedimentation chamber.
    b   Sedgewick-Rafter cell, with coverslip in diagonal position for filling the cell.

is powdered and applied to the joint in the form of a slurry in water and the chamber is then heated to 550 °C for 15 to 30 min. The seal is good but will, in time, be affected by the use of acidic solutions. The above method is the one currently in favour at this laboratory but details of the use of other cements, including epoxy-resins, are provided by Lund, Kipling & Le Cren (1958). Alternatively, measuring cylinders may be used as sedimentation chambers. The excess liquid is siphoned off and the remaining material transferred (with care!) to a counting chamber. Such a transfer may be necessary if nannoplankters are to be counted.

The most commonly used method involves the addition of a preservative to the water sample in the chamber, in the ratio of 1 to 100, to speed the sedimentation process. For phytoplankton the preservative is usually Lugol's solution (10 g I_2, 20 g KI, 200 ml distilled water; add 20 g glacial acetic acid a few days before use; store in the dark) although this is not suitable for all organisms. Alternatively the addition of 0·2 ml of each of 5% Tween 80, 40% formaldehyde and 20% copper sulphate to each 100 ml of sample may prove satisfactory. It is important to allow sufficient time for even the smallest microbes to settle (allow 3 h for each centimetre of chamber height). The whole area of the chamber is usually scanned for larger organisms, since their distribution is not always random. Smaller organisms may be counted either on a transect or as described below. Details of the counting procedure are provided by Lund, Kipling & Le Cren (1958) and are briefly as follows. Three 'hairs' are fixed in the eyepiece; two are parallel and a convenient distance apart and the third is at right angles to them and lying across the middle of the field of view. The 'hairs' are actually glass threads, made by drawing out molten glass, and are cemented to a cardboard, cork or brass ring which is made to fit inside the eyepiece. The eyepiece is rotated in the microscope until the parallel hairs are horizontal, and the whole of the base of the sedimentation tube is covered by traversing backwards and forwards. The algae are counted as they pass the vertical hair and at the end of a transect the field is moved vertically by a distance equal to that between the parallel hairs. Algae lying across the upper hair are counted as in the field of view; those on the lower hair are not counted since they will be included in the next transect.

Microscopy is usually confined to the use of low-power objectives when the basic sedimentation chamber is used, but modifications are available which allow the use of conventional microscopy for counting smaller organisms. Most such modifications of the chamber consist of a cylinder which slides off the basal plate, removing the bulk of the liquid and leaving the sedimented material undisturbed in a shallow well sunk into the base (Evans 1972). A coverslip may then be placed over the well and the organisms counted by transmitted or incident light microscopy.

4.2.2 *The Sedgewick – Rafter cell*

This is a slide (usually made of plastic) with a rectangular raised rim on its upper surface, such that, when a coverslip is placed over the area enclosed by the rim, the cell holds 1 ml. The cell has a depth of 1 mm and it is ruled into 1000 units each of 1 mm². The accuracy of the total volume enclosed in the cell may be determined by weight. If the volume involved is too large or the detritus component of the sample too great for a chamber of such depth to be used, the raised rim may be ground down to, say, half its depth. Such chambers are useful for counting larger microorganisms, particularly the slower-moving ciliated protozoa. Although it is possible to obtain reproducible and accurate results if the contents of the cell are determined by weight, great care must be taken in filling the chamber if it is to be assumed that it contains its nominal volume (i.e. 1 ml). This is best achieved by placing the coverslip diagonally across the chamber (Fig. 4b), introducing the sample with a piston pipette through the gap at one corner while air is expelled at the opposite corner. The coverslip is then rotated carefully to enclose the sample.

Smaller organisms (e.g. phytoplankton) may also be counted, using an eyepiece graticule, but a higher-power objective of long working distance will be required. Thus, a wide variety of counting procedures are possible with the Sedgewick-Rafter cell, ranging from counting the whole contents to sub-sampling very small areas. Each approach has its limitations and problems; these are discussed in section 4.7.

4.3 SIMPLE CHAMBERS WHICH MAY BE MADE IN THE LABORATORY

Fairly simple counting chambers may be made in the laboratory if alternatives to the commercial products are required. Algal sedimentation chambers might be included in this category.

4.3.1 *Moat chamber for larger microorganisms*

In this laboratory a circular open flat-bottomed moat is cut in perspex with a barrier at one point along its length (Fig. 5a). The chamber is attached to a clamp so that it may be fixed to, and rotated on, a conventional light-microscope stage or a stereo-microscope. The sample is dispensed into the moat, the chamber is rotated on its central spindle and the organisms are counted along the length of the moat using the barrier as starting and finishing point. Many variants on this theme are possible, including straight moats in rectangular blocks of perspex. The depth of the moat and

the volume of sample which it will hold are dictated by the requirements of the individual.   The chamber is particularly useful for larger organisms, e.g. larger ciliates or meiobenthos.

4.3.2   *Lund chamber* (Lund 1959)

This consists of a coverslip, usually 22×50 mm, cemented along its longer sides to strips of coverslip cut to the same length.   The strips are then cemented to a slide thus forming a chamber (Fig.5b) with open ends, as long as the slide and as wide as the gap between the strips.   The strips are cut with a diamond pencil and may be cemented with an epoxy-resin.   Alternatively the coverslip is cemented with glass solder.   The solder crystals are melted in a suitable metal crucible and threads of the molten glass are drawn out with a metal needle.   When they have set, two threads of the solder glass are used to support the coverslip along the longer sides on the slide.   A strip of coverslip, as thick as the required depth of the chamber but longer than the coverslip of the chamber, is placed between the slide and the coverslip.   The chamber is then baked at 550-560 °C for 15-30 min during which the glass solder threads melt and the coverslip settles on the underlying glass strip.   The slide is allowed to cool and the central glass strip is removed.   The solidified solder now acts as the outer walls of the chamber.   The volume of the sample contained in the chamber may be determined from the area and mean depth, or from its weight.   The coverslip may be fixed, as described above, and the chamber filled by capillarity, or it may be loose and placed carefully on a drop of sample on the slide.   The depth of the chamber will depend on the size of the organisms and the required depth of field.   This chamber is often used to count μ-algae after transfer from a sedimentation chamber, and at least one version is available commercially, from the Water Research Centre.

4.3.3   *Marked slide* (Trolldenier 1973)

A known area is marked, usually as a circle, on a glass slide.   A sample of known volume is dispensed on this area and allowed to dry.   Care must be taken to ensure even distribution of the material and this is helped by the addition of a small quantity of dispersant (e.g. sodium hexa-metaphosphate at a final concentration of $0 \cdot 0005$ to $0 \cdot 01\%$) and the use of a flat bench.   Dispersants are best avoided if fluorochromes are to be used because they increase the background fluorescence.   Addition of agar at a final concentration of $0 \cdot 1\%$ ensures adhesion of the material to the slide.   Trolldenier (1973) provides details of this technique and recommends marking the slide with an outer and inner circle of $11 \cdot 3$ mm diameter ($\equiv 1$ cm^2) and $7 \cdot 72$ mm diameter.   The outer edge of the inner circle corresponds to the region of average thickness of the

clamping point to microscope stage   barrier

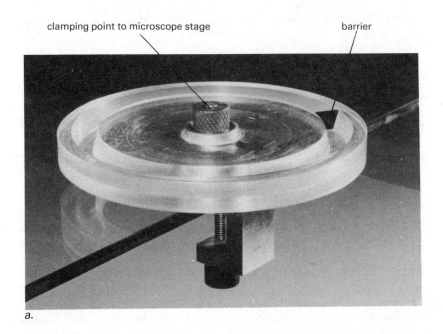

a.

b.

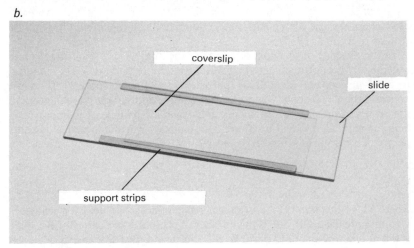

Fig. 5a   Moat chambers for larger organisms.
      b   Lund chambers for smaller organisms.

smear.   Trolldenier used 10 μl aliquots of soil dilutions, dispensed with a piston pipette, but the method is also suitable for benthic material.

4.4   COUNTING WITHOUT CHAMBERS

Fairly accurate counts may be obtained by very simple procedures. Algae may be counted by covering a known small volume of sample with a square coverslip and counting transects.   Details of this method are given by Edmondson (1974).   Larger organisms (e.g. benthic ciliates) may be counted in drops of known size on a glass plate or slide (e.g. Goulder 1971; Finlay, Laybourn & Strachan 1979).   The coverslip method may be adapted for counts of specific groups of bacteria.   Caldwell & Tiedje (1975a), for example, counted photosynthetic bacteria by placing drops of sample on dried agar on slides and covering immediately with a cover slip.   The agar absorbed the water (the bacteria being thus deposited in a single plane) and an improved phase-contrast image was obtained.   The rectangular cross-sectioned capillaries developed by Perfilev & Gabe (1969) are now available commercially and may be used as counting chambers.   Careful calibration will be necessary to obtain quantitative data, but comparative information may be obtained quite readily.   An early example of the use of capillaries to enumerate bacterioplankton is given by Collins & Kipling (1957).

In the absence of any sort of chamber the number of organisms may be obtained by proportional counting with an internal standard.   The standard is a suspension of identifiable particles (e.g. fungal spores) of known concentration.   Known volumes of the sample and standard are mixed and the relative numbers of organisms and standard particles per microscope field (or any suitable unit area) are determined.   The number of organisms per ml of the original sample n_o is given by

$$n_o = \frac{O_f \cdot [\text{SP}] \, V_{SP}}{SP_f \cdot V_o}$$

where O_f is the number of organisms per microscope field (or whatever counting area is used), SP_f is the number of standard particles per field, $[SP]$ is the number of standard particles ml^{-1} in the original suspension, V_o is the volume of the sample (ml) and V_{SP} the volume of the standard particle suspension (ml).

4.5 MICROSCOPY

Sedimentation chambers for larger plankton may be examined directly on the inverted microscope under the equivalent of bright field illumination.   Many of the chambers and their cover glasses are so thick that objectives of long working-distance may be necessary. If thin coverslips are used (e.g. in the Helber chamber or some of the simple chambers) then phase contrast microscopy may be employed, but such coverslips may increase the errors due to variability of chamber depth (4.1.2a).   Material may be examined in the unstained state or, if improved resolution is required, bright field stains such as phenolic erythrosine (3.4.2) or fluorochromes (3.4.3) may be used.   Special eyepiece graticules may be useful if counts of filamentous organisms are undertaken (see Sections 4.6 and 6.3.3).

4.6 THE ORGANISMS

The decision on whether to count individual cells in colonial forms, or to count the number of colonies and multiply by a mean value for cell number, is largely dictated by the questions being asked and the precision required of the answers.   This applies to membrane counts as well, except that there is more likely to be disruption of colonies during filtration.   Likewise, when filamentous bacteria, algae and fungi are encountered, some consideration must be given to the most useful units of enumeration.   Numbers of filaments may be misleading if considerable variability in length is observed.   It may be necessary to measure, or at least to size-class, the filaments.   To obtain biomass estimates, details of filament length and width are required, although direct measurement may be replaced by counting the number of times the filaments intersect a calibrated graticule (see Section 6.3.3).

The size and population density of the organisms will largely govern the counting chamber used.   Phytoplankton are usually counted in sedimentation chambers or smaller counting chambers.   Protozoa (at least the larger species) may be counted in a variety of open or closed chambers.   Fungi are more frequently enumerated by viable count procedures (see Chapter 5) although there is no theoretical reason why, after suitable concentration of the material, direct counts should not be attempted by one of the above methods.   The numerous small phyto- and zooflagellates often encountered, particularly in benthic material, may be counted in a haemocytometer or similar chamber.   Bacteria are usually counted on membranes, although the Trolldenier slide technique (4.3.3) has certain attractions for benthic material.   A summary guide to counting procedures for the different groups of microorganisms is given in 4.9.

4.7 ANALYSIS OF RESULTS

The number of organisms per unit volume of the original sample (n_1) is given by

$$n_1 = \frac{\bar{Y}_1 d}{v}$$

where $\bar{Y}_1$ is the mean count per graticule area, v is the volume represented by that area and d is the dilution or concentration factor applied to the sample.

The parent distribution of the counts, however, must be determined before confidence limits or parametric statistical tests can be applied to the mean (Elliott 1977; see also Appendix A).

Cassell (1965) produced a series of graphs which allowed 90-99% confidence limits of counts of dried films or in chambers to be calculated from the mean and the number of fields. Or, in reverse, the number of organisms required to achieve a particular confidence interval could be chosen. These graphs assume a random distribution of organisms, and, therefore, this will have to be checked before they can be used. There is evidence, however, that the distribution of organisms will vary considerably in such chambers (Poisson, logarithmic, negative binomial) depending on the amount of particulate material and the degree of aggregation of the organisms (Jones, Mollison & Quenouille 1948).

Lund, Kipling & Le Cren (1958) have demonstrated that counts on samples and sub-samples in sedimentation tubes follow a random distribution, the errors of which are small relative to the sampling error.

A variety of distributions have been reported for the Sedgewick-Rafter cell. Woelkerling et al. (1976) examined the errors involved in its use for phytoplankton counts. They concluded that organisms should be allowed to settle (they were counting preserved samples) and that the settling time (15 min is usually recommended) depended on the type of preservation. Counting random micrometer fields was preferred to strip-counting across the cell and greater accuracy was obtained by making fewer counts on a larger number of cells. The parent distribution of the data varied so much, however, that non-parametric statistical techniques were recommended for comparison of samples.

The distribution of phytoplankton in the slide-coverslip chamber of Lund (1959), of ciliated protozoa in sub-sample drops and a moat chamber (Goulder 1971, 1975; Finlay, Laybourn & Strachan 1979), and of bacteria on a marked slide (Trolldenier 1973) all conformed to a Poisson model. Benthic ciliates in 0·1 ml samples counted under a coverslip exhibited a contagious distribution and required a logarithmic transformation (Goulder 1974).

If one of the simple methods described in 4·3 or 4·4 is being used then either all the organisms in the chamber should be counted or it must be confirmed that the apparent distribution pattern holds for the whole area of the chamber or slide. In particular, it is important to check for higher densities of organisms at the edges of coverslips, etc. It is possible to obtain counts from transects but the results may be of comparative rather than absolute value.

It is evident from the above that the parent distribution of microbial counts in chambers will vary with the organism, the degree of aggregation and the type of chamber. In view of the paucity of quantitative data in some areas of freshwater microbiology, particularly from benthic samples, the reader is strongly advised to check the distribution for each sampling or counting regime used.

4.8 AUTORADIOGRAPHIC, FLUORESCENT ANTIBODY AND CYTOCHEMICAL METHODS

Where information is required about the capacity of organisms to assimilate particular substrates, micro-autoradiographic methods may be used. Particular species in a sample may be counted directly, if certain conditions are met, by a fluorescent antibody technique. Biochemical activity in the cell may be detected by cytochemical techniques and active organisms may be observed, and sometimes counted, under the microscope. It is beyond the scope of this book to provide details of these methods, but they may be used in conjunction with direct-count techniques; a guide to the literature is included here.

4.8.1 *Micro-autoradiography*

Exposure of silver halide to radioactive substances will produce an image in the form of silver grains. This is the basis of autoradiography. Samples are exposed to a radioactive substrate and then covered with a fine-grain photographic emulsion. Radioactivity within the organisms is detected as superimposed silver grains. The method may be used to distinguish active from inactive cells and even to determine growth rate.

^{14}C substrates may be used, including $^{14}CO_2$, which could provide an estimate of autotrophic carbon fixation, but tritium remains the most favoured isotope. This is because the energy emitted is weak and therefore tracklength is short, providing good resolution. More recently ^{32}P substrates, or the softer ^{33}P isotope, have also been used. The sample is exposed to the substrate, usually of high specific activity, and then after the

TABLE 2. SOURCE REFERENCES TO THE APPLICATION OF
AUTORADIOGRAPHIC TECHNIQUES IN MICROBIAL ECOLOGY

References	Isotopes	Experimental Conditions	
Bowie & Gillespie (1976)	^{14}C ^{3}H	M,S	E
Faust & Correll (1977)	^{14}C ^{33}P	S	E
Fliermans & Schmidt (1975)	^{14}C	S	E
Fry & Humphrey (1978)	^{3}H	S	E
Hoppe (1976)	^{3}H	M	F
Iturriaga & Hoppe (1977)	^{14}C	M	F
Meyer-Reil (1978)	^{3}H	M	E
Munro & Brock (1968)	^{14}C ^{3}H	S	E
Paerl (1974)	^{3}H	M	E
Paerl (1977)	^{3}H	M	E
Paerl & Goldman (1972)	^{14}C	M	E
Paerl & Lean (1976)	^{33}P	M	E
Paerl & Williams (1976)	^{14}C	M	E
Peroni & Lavarello (1975)	^{32}P	M	F
Ramsay (1974)	^{3}H	S	E
Ramsay & Fry (1976)	^{3}H	S	E
Stanley & Staley (1977)	^{3}H	S	E
Waid et al. (1973)	^{14}C	S	E

M = organisms concentrated on a membrane filter

S = organisms concentrated (e.g. by centrifugation) and then smeared on a glass slide

E = liquid emulsion used for exposure

F = photographic film used for exposure.

reaction is stopped with Lugol's iodine, formaldehyde or glutaraldehyde, a concentrate of the organisms is smeared on a glass slide. Adhesion is usually enhanced by the use of gelatin or Ullrich's adhesive. It is also possible to prepare autoradiograms of membrane-filtered material and although the image thus obtained was originally less satisfactory, recent improvements in methodology have overcome this problem. The slide with the smear or cleared membrane is then dipped in photographic emulsion, usually a fine-grain liquid nuclear emulsion (Kodak NTB-2), or placed in contact with fine-grain photographic film, exposed for several days and then processed. The material may be treated with a biological stain so that small organisms such as bacteria which have not taken up radioactive substrate may also be seen.

The method is particularly useful in providing information about the rate of uptake of the specific substrate used. If that substrate is $^{14}CO_2$, then some useful general information about primary production may be obtained; but since heterotrophic organisms rarely use a single unique substrate it is not possible to obtain the same amount of information about total heterotrophic production. Autoradiography is particularly useful for studying associations and the transfer of material between microbes which live in close proximity.

The autoradiographic procedure used at this laboratory for cell smears and membranes is essentially that of Meyer-Reil (1978); further details of methodology are provided by Brock & Brock (1968). References to more recent applications in microbial ecology and to innovations in methodology are summarized in Table 2. Details of a quantitative (track auto-radiography) approach are provided by Knoechel & Kalff (1976) and a combined epifluorescence-autoradiographic method by Meyer-Reil (1978).

4.8.2 *Fluorescent antibody technique*

This method provides a good estimate of viable populations in autecological studies, in that it allows observation and identification of the organism in a single step. Much of the published work to date has been concerned with soil populations, where valuable information has been gained on the dynamics of specific fungal and bacterial populations.

The microorganism under study is isolated in pure culture and then a preparation of whole cells or some part of the cell (e.g. the cell wall) is injected into a laboratory animal to produce the antibodies. When the antibody titre reaches its maximum, the blood is fractionated and the antibodies are purified and tagged with a suitable fluorochrome, usually fluorescein isothiocyanate (FITC). When added to a sample, the antibody reacts with the antigenic microorganisms, if any are present, causing them to fluoresce. Quantitative estimates in fresh or fixed preparations can be made on slides or membrane filters, either by counting, using incident light illumination, or with a suitable fluorimetric apparatus if background levels of interference allow. The filter combinations required for FITC fluorescence are often similar to those used for acridine fluorochromes (see section 3.4.3), i.e. excitation with blue light and emission in the green region.

The method is confined to single-species or autecological studies but provides valuable information as long as the necessary rigorous control tests are observed. Among these the most important is that for specificity of the

antibody, that it reacts only with the original antigenic organism. The procedures for conducting such control tests are summarized by Schmidt (1973), who also includes a list of published applications of the method to ecological samples.

Apart from other organisms which may interfere because of cross-reactions, there is also the possibility of non-specific adsorption of the fluorescent antibody to organic matter or detritus. This may be overcome by pretreatment with a different fluorochrome, usually rhodamine tagged to gelatin. This occupies the active sites in the samples and, after addition of the FITC- antibody, the organisms are seen to fluoresce green against a red background (Bohlool & Schmidt 1968).

Examples of application of fluorescence antibody technique in aquatic microbiology, with some details of the methods used are given by Belly, Bohlool & Brock (1973), Bohlool & Brock (1974) and Strayer & Tiedje (1978). The method may also be combined with micro-autoradiography to determine which individuals of a particular species are metabolically active (Fliermans & Schmidt 1975).

4.8.3 *Cytochemical methods*

There appears to have been a resurgence of interest in the use of tetrazolium salts as cytochemical stains, particularly for bacteria. Patriquin & Dobereiner (1978) used triphenyltetrazolium chloride for the direct examination of rhizosphere bacteria. Iturriaga & Rheinheimer (1975) used 2–(p–iodophenyl)–3–(p–nitrophenyl)–5–phenyl tetrazolium chloride (INT) to examine planktonic and benthic bacteria. The tetrazolium salts are reduced to their corresponding coloured formazans by the electron transport systems of the organisms. A diffuse coloration is usually observed in eukaryotes, but respiring prokaryotes produce optically-dense red spots in the cells. The above authors included a substrate in the incubation mixture, but Zimmermann, Iturriaga & Becker-Birck (1978) obtained good results with planktonic bacteria using INT alone, in a technique which combined the cytochemical method with an epifluorescence count. Our results with freshwater bacteria indicate that the highest quality bright-field optics must be used to obtain satisfactory resolution of the formazan spots. We have had some success in combining the INT and Acridine Orange method with the nalidixic acid inhibition technique of Kogure, Simidu & Taga (1979). Nalidixic acid inhibits prokaryotic DNA synthesis and when it is added to the water sample (final concentration 20 mg 1^{-1}) which has been enriched with yeast extract (final concentration

250 mg l^{-1}) a proportion of the viable bacteria grow but are unable to divide. The organisms become enlarged and elongated and are easily resolved by bright-field, phase-contrast or fluorescence microscopy. Further tests are required but preliminary results indicate that a much higher viable count is obtained by this method than by any conventional viable-count technique (see section 5).

Fluorescein diacetate and methyl fluorescein phosphate may be used as cytochemical substrates to detect the presence of membrane-bound hydrolytic enzymes. Details of the procedure and some reservations on their use are given in section 3.4.3. More information is required on the efficiency of cytochemical methods, particularly with regard to the potential inhibitory effects of tetrazolium salts (see section 5.2.5, a(ii)).

4.9 A SUMMARY GUIDE TO DIRECT COUNTS OF FRESHWATER MICROORGANISMS

Methods for counting the major groups of microorganisms, in the plankton and the benthos, are summarized in Table 3 (p. 50). An alternative is offered for each, but these methods should not be regarded as the recommended first and second choice for every occasion. The individual researcher must remain the best judge of the most suitable approach for any particular problem. Due to the paucity of information on direct counts of fungi (with the exception of those which are parasitic on algae) the methods offered should be considered as extremely tentative. Consideration will have to be given to the accuracy and the precision required (see Appendix A), before embarking on a programme of counting. It is likely, for example, that membrane filters will allow work to a higher degree of precision (i.e. the counts will have smaller confidence limits) but counts may be lower on the membrane due to cell breakage, penetration or loss of resolution for some other reason.

TABLE 3.   A SUMMARY GUIDE TO DIRECT COUNTS OF
FRESHWATER MICROORGANISMS

Organism	Source	Method	Micro-scopy	Relevant Section
Algae	Plankton	(a) Sedimentation chamber	I	4.2.1
		(b) Other chambers	B	4.1 or 4.3.2
	Benthos[1]	(a) Chamber	B	4.2.2 4.3.2
		(b) Membrane	F	3.2.3 3.4.3
Bacteria	Plankton	(a) Membrane	F	3.4.3
		(b) Membrane	B	3.4.2
	Benthos	(a) Membrane	F	3.4.3
		(b) Marked slide acridine or erythrosine	F or B	4.3.3
Fungi	Plankton	Chamber count after concentration	B	2.2 4.1
	Benthos	Marked slide/erythrosine	B	4.3.3
Protozoa	Plankton	(a) Moat chamber (large)	B	4.3.1 2.2
		(b) Chamber count after concentration (small)	B	4.1
	Benthos	(a) Simple chambers	B	4.3
		(b) Sedgewick – Rafter cell	B	4.2.2

[1] An attempt should be made to count haptobenthos directly by epifluorescence.
I = inverted   B = bright field   F = fluorescence.

5. COUNTING VIABLE ORGANISMS

5.1 INTRODUCTION

The viability of microorganisms in a sample is assessed by testing their capacity to grow and divide, if necessary until visible growth occurs. The result is then usually referred to as the *viable count* to distinguish it from the total or direct count obtained by the methods in sections 3 and 4. This term may not be grammatically correct but has the advantages of being concise and readily understood by microbiologists, and therefore is used in this text. The problems associated with the two types of counting are summarized in section 1.

To obtain viable counts, the organisms are provided with sources of carbon and energy and then incubated, either for a few cell-divisions or until sufficient growth has occurred for observations to be made with the naked eye. The methods are most often applied to bacteria but may be used successfully under certain circumstances to count algae, fungi and protozoa. They may be used to obtain an estimate of total viable numbers of a large group (e.g. bacteria), or employed in some selective capacity to enumerate a particular genus, species or sub-group (e.g. coliforms or cellulose decomposers). The latter approach usually yields more accurate results, partly because the efficiency of recovery of the method can be tested in the laboratory. The problems associated with 'total-viable' counts are well known, and most revolve around the fact that whatever growth medium is used will always exert selective pressures. Only a part of the population, therefore, will grow, and the size of this fraction will depend on the manipulative methods used before incubation (dilution procedures etc.), the medium, and the period and conditions of incubation.

The literature abounds with details of methods, media etc.; the basic principles and quantitative aspects of the methods are included here. References to suitable media are included in section 5.2.5.

Viable counting methods may be divided into two broad categories: (a) those which count discrete units of single species in colonies (*colony counts*); (b) those involving dilution to extinction, followed by growth of mixed cultures at chosen dilutions (*Most Probable Number* or *MPN counts*).

5.2 COLONY COUNTS

5.2.1 *Plate counts*

The nutrient medium is solidified to a gel using agar, gelatin or silica gel. Agar is by far the easiest to use, but silica gel may be necessary for nutritionally-demanding organisms or for the growth of chemolithotrophs. The medium is dispensed into petri dishes and an aliquot of a suitable dilution of the sample is applied and either mixed before the agar sets (*pour plates*), or spread on the surface of the agar with a sterile glass rod or wire (*spread plates*). Pour plates are used less frequently for ecological work, largely because sensitive organisms are killed at the temperature of the molten agar.

The sample may be diluted in a separate vessel and shaken vigorously to ensure even distribution of the organisms. If the dilution required to produce countable plates is not too great (e.g. spreading $0 \cdot 1$ ml of a 10^{-1} dilution), as with counts of planktonic bacteria, the dilution steps may be omitted. A smaller volume of sample ($10 \, \mu l$), dispensed from a suitable piston pipette directly into a drop of diluent on the plate, may be spread immediately. The diluent merely provides bulk and allows the small sample volume to be spread over the whole plate. Apart from the fact that the method is quicker, counts obtained have been higher (although less precise) than those from conventional dilution procedures (Jones 1973b).

5.2.2 *Drop plate method*

This is a modification of the plate count technique developed by Miles & Misra (1938) and may be used in similar circumstances. A series of drops (6 or more depending on their size) of a suitable dilution of the sample are spotted on the agar plate and allowed to dry in. The plates are incubated and the number of micro-colonies which develop in the drop area are counted. The advantages over the conventional plating procedure are speed and economy, against which has to be balanced the fact that the method is usually suitable only for counts of bacteria. Bousefield et al. (1973) obtained good precision when the drops were dispensed from a piston pipette, and the results compared favourably with spread plate counts, but these trials were conducted with pure cultures of bacteria.

Surface colony counts may be hampered by the presence of bacteria which produce spreading colonies and inhibit other bacteria on the plate (these are common in fresh water). The spreading growth is not easily inhibited and therefore the only solution at present is to have enough replicate plates (ten is usually sufficient) for those containing spreaders to be discarded. A count of the spreading bacteria on ten plates will allow their number per unit volume to be calculated and incorporated in the viable count.

5.2.3 Membrane filter methods

A known volume of sample, or a dilution thereof (for sediments), is filtered through a membrane which is then incubated either on an absorbent pad (e.g. glass fibre or cellulose filter pads) soaked in a suitable liquid medium, or directly on an agar plate. The micro-colonies which develop may be counted at the early stage with a microscope (e.g. after 5 or 6 cell divisions), or later when they are visible to the naked eye. The objections to the use of growth media still apply, and the effect of the membrane filter on organisms and their recovery should also be considered. The membrane filters which have been developed for the recovery of faecal bacteria are worthy of consideration in this context (Green et al. 1975; Lin 1976). Their graded pore structure ($2 \cdot 5 \mu m$ pore-opening tapering down to a $0 \cdot 7 \mu m$ pore) ensures a more gentle filtration. We have obtained higher yields of particle-bound enzymes, and higher viable counts of certain heterotrophs, with these membranes and it may be that, in spite of their larger nominal pore size, they could be more efficient in the recovery of viable organisms from water.

The micro-colonies may be examined on unstained membranes by phase-contrast microscopy, or stained and examined under bright field illumination. Small micro-colonies (a few cells) may be stained as in section 3.4.2, but for larger colonies (low-power or stereo-microscopy) staining for 30 min with 1% aqueous erythrosine (Collins et al. 1973) or $0 \cdot 1$–1% aqueous methylene blue (Niemelä 1965) is adequate. Decolorization follows the procedure in section 3.4.2.

The main advantage of membrane filters over conventional plating procedures is in their use when numbers of organisms are very low. The concentration and inoculation stages are thus completed in a single step, but the counts obtained are usually lower than plate counts.

The recently-described technique of counting enlarged and elongated bacteria on membranes after nalidixic acid inhibition (Kogure, Simidu & Toga 1979; see Section 4.8.3) is worthy of further examination.

5.2.4 Slide culture

This method is normally used for the determination of percentage viability in pure cultures (Postgate 1969), but may provide more reliable information on 'viability' of aquatic bacteria, as long as it is remembered that the disadvantages associated with the choice of medium still apply. The agar medium is membrane-filtered while hot, and then dispensed into stainless steel or plastic rings on a glass slide. The volume is usually $0 \cdot 20$–$0 \cdot 25$ ml, depending on the rings used. When the agar is dry it is inoculated with a loop of the sample population. Planktonic samples, in particular, will have to be concentrated before inoculation, since the method requires 5×10^7 to

5×10^8 organisms per ml to provide an adequate number of organisms per microscope field.   The ring is sealed to a coverslip with water and incubated for long enough to allow 2 or 3 cell divisions.   The number of micro-colonies and individual cells is then counted and the percentage viability determined.   Once suitable incubation temperatures and times have been established, the method may provide more accurate information on viability, since it requires the cell to perform only 1 or 2 divisions rather than produce a visible colony.   Because of the small volumes used it might also be possible to use media which more closely resemble the natural environment (e.g. concentrated lake water).   The organisms are usually counted by phase contrast microscopy, the image of which is improved by the agar medium.

5.2.5   *The organisms and media*

Colony count methods have been used most frequently for the estimation of bacterial populations but, with minor modifications (usually to the growth medium), comparative data for the other major microbial groups may be obtained.

a. Bacteria: two nutrient media which have been used successfully in the past are Casein-Peptone-Starch agar (CPS) for freshwater bacteria (Taylor 1940; Collins & Willoughby 1962; Jones 1970) and Casitone-Glycerol-Yeast Extract agar (CGY) for sewage and polluted water (Pike et al. 1972).   Johnston & Cross (1976) provide details of a modification of the colloidal chitin agar used for actinomycetes.   Details of other more complex formulations are provided by Collins et al. (1973).   A wide variety of specific growth media and special recipes exists, and many of these are given by Skerman (1969) and Aaronson (1970).   If a high degree of replication or miniaturization is required then Hartmann (1968) should be consulted.   Many of the media are selective, through the incorporation of either inhibitors or specific substrates.   The latter may be used to detect microorganisms with particular metabolic capabilities in one of two ways.

(i) Detection of products released by the organisms into the medium. Examples include: the release of exoenzymes which produce distinct zones around colonies; the release of end products such as acid and gas (the former may be detected by inclusion of a pH indicator in the medium); and the ability to degrade specific polymers (e.g. starch).   Such tests may be applied to both plate and MPN counts, and to a lesser degree to membrane counts.

(ii) Detection of particular enzymes in the cell or colonies, e.g. the test for phosphatase by spraying colonies with a-naphthyl phosphate and observing the colour change.

Caution should be exercised in the addition of electron acceptors to media

to increase the visibility of the bacterial growth in plates or in MPN procedures (Bochner & Savageau 1977). Although satisfactory results may be obtained with pure cultures, inhibition of aquatic bacteria by tetrazolium salts has been observed in this laboratory and by others (Niemelä 1965).

Those interested in enumerating bacterial indicators of faecal pollution are referred to the Ministry of Housing and Local Government (1969) Report 71 and American Public Health Association (1976). The former is in the process of being updated under the auspices of the Department of the Environment and the Department of Health and Social Security. A valuable contribution to the debate on the use of indicator organisms, which includes a detailed statistical argument, is provided by Bonde (1977). Developments in the field of water quality monitoring are rapid and the reader who wishes to keep abreast of recent advances is referred to the review edition (the sixth number each year) of *Journal of the Water Pollution Control Federation*.

b. Algae which are capable of growth on agar may be plated-out, but this method is usually confined to studies of pure cultures rather than natural populations. Fragile algae would be unlikely to withstand the shock of the plating procedure. Examples of media which might be used are Chu 10 (Chu 1942) for more demanding algae and those requiring silica, and ASM 1 (Gorham et al. 1964) as a general medium not containing silica.

c. Fungi, particularly those from soils, are often estimated by plate count procedures. The method has distinct disadvantages for this purpose in that it is reputed to select for germination of spores while not encouraging the growth of vegetative hyphae. The count thus obtained may, therefore, be more representative of resting stages than of the growing population. In addition, many aquatic phycomycetes do not grow (or at least cannot be isolated) by this technique, which is more appropriate for members of the Fungi Imperfecti. Aquatic fungi are therefore best estimated by enrichment or baiting techniques (see Section 5.3.2) or by direct observations on the substratum. If, however, plating techniques are to be used then media containing polymers such as chitin or cellulose, inhibitors such as tellurite, and antibiotics such as penicillin and streptomycin often prove to be the most successful. Details of these and other techniques are provided by Jones (1971).

d. Protozoa are often too fragile to withstand plating procedures and MPN procedures are usually preferred (see Section 5.3). Under certain circumstances, however, bacteriolytic populations, particularly amoebae, may be estimated by inoculation on lawn plates of a bacterial prey. The protozoans form plaques which may provide an estimate of the population

size, but microscopic examination is necessary to avoid confusion with plaques formed by bacteriophage and bacterial parasites such as *Bdellovibrio* spp. Details of suitable media are given by Page (1976).

5.2.6 *Analysis of results*

The normal procedures for determination of the distribution pattern and choice of suitable transformation for counts will apply (see Appendix A), but one or two additional factors must be taken into consideration. Most viable count procedures involve dilution of the sample. If no errors are attached to the dilution procedure, and if the organisms are not clumped and are unaffected by the dilution, then the count on a 10^{-1} dilution should be one-tenth of that of the undiluted sample. This is very rarely the case, and it is left to the individual researcher to decide which procedure to adopt. The choice is usually between working to a fixed dilution and counting a wide range of colonies per plate, or attempting to choose an acceptable range of numbers per plate and therefore using a series of dilutions. In the latter case the researcher must choose the dilution which provides the 'best' count, and may accept this as an estimate of the mean, or may incorporate results from other dilutions to obtain a weighted mean. If a single dilution is used, the problem is one of deciding what are acceptable limits for the total number of colonies per plate. The oft-quoted range of 30-300 colonies per plate still has a considerable following for little logical reason (Niemelä 1965). Under such circumstances the counts are often log-normally distributed, whereas if the counts are in the range of 40-60 colonies per plate (as recommended by Postgate (1969) and discussed in more detail by Jones (1970)) then they often conform to a Poisson distribution. Fisher et al. (1922), in a detailed study of colony dispersion, concluded that under 'ideal' conditions a Poisson distribution will be obtained. If there was antagonism between the organisms or a defect in the growth medium, then there was a respective increase or decrease in the sample variance. Jones (1973a) published factors from which confidence limits of geometric means of bacterial plate counts can be calculated for populations from 10^2 ml^{-1} to 10^5 ml^{-1}.

Badger & Pankhurst (1960) observed a Poisson distribution of micro-colonies in surface drops, although the results obtained by Bousefield et al. (1973) indicate a somewhat smaller variance. Colony counts on membrane filters may also be distributed randomly (Jones 1973b) although the use of gridded membranes may cause a deviation from the Poisson (Niemelä 1965).

The advent of more precise instruments for the delivery of small volumes (e.g. piston pipettes), and other changes in technique, will affect the

distribution of the data obtained. It is therefore unwise to assume parity with results reported in the literature.

5.3 MOST PROBABLE NUMBER (MPN) COUNTS

5.3.1 *Experimental procedure*

A series of dilutions of the sample is prepared and a number of aliquots from each dilution is inoculated into or on to the growth medium. The inoculated medium is incubated and then growth is recorded as the number of positive scores at each dilution. The method is based on successive dilution of the sample until some inocula contain no organisms. The degree of dilution required and the number of positive scores at different levels of dilution are used to obtain the MPN of organisms in the sample by reference to suitable tables. It is, of course, impossible to tell whether growth originates from one organism or more, or whether, indeed, a single organism is capable of producing growth. The statistical argument which is used to produce the tables of MPNs is actually based on the negative scores and the sample must be diluted sufficiently to bring the results within the range of the tables.

Most MPN methods use liquid media, and a positive score is recorded when the medium is turbid with growth. This is not essential, however, and regions of agar plates may be similarly inoculated and surface growth noted (Harris & Sommers 1968). Counts obtained with MPN methods are often higher than those from conventional plating procedures. This is sometimes attributed to the fact that organisms are not separated into discrete colonies, and the interactions which normally occur in the field are therefore continued in the artificial medium. Although higher counts may be obtained, the confidence limits which can be placed on these are often much wider than those on plate counts. The range of these limits may be reduced by increasing the number of replicates at each dilution, or by reducing the dilution factor; but if different volumes rather than equal volumes of different dilutions are used, then the precision will depend on the maximum and minimum volumes used (Meynell & Meynell 1970; Melchiorri-Santolini 1972). Details of the effect of these factors on the confidence limits obtained, and references to suitable tables, are given in 5.3.3.

The MPN method has been used most frequently in conjunction with highly selective media (e.g. for indicator bacteria) and a tenfold dilution series, usually in test tubes. Tables for this dilution ratio with five replicates at each dilution are most common, but this should not discourage the use of a lower dilution ratio and greater replication to increase precision.

Miniaturization may also reduce the manipulation time.   Plastic micro-titre dishes (8×12 well design) are ideal and have been used successfully, in this laboratory for a fourfold dilution series with a multiple-tip piston pipette (inoculating $50\,\mu l$ into $150\,\mu l$), and by Rowe et al. (1977) for a twofold dilution series using calibrated loops.

The manipulative aspects of MPN methodology present very few difficulties but the choice of MPN tables and the method of scoring may cause some confusion and are dealt with in some detail in section 5.3.3.

5.3.2   *The organisms and media*

The MPN method requires no special media, and any of those referred to in 5.2.5 would be suitable.   Liquid media are usually preferred since, it is argued, these allow more organism interaction and are less likely to create stress than solid media.

The treatment of microbes in the MPN technique may, therefore, be much less harsh than procedures involving plating or the use of membrane filters.   It is likely to be more suitable for delicate organisms, and although MPN methods have been used largely for bacteria they have also been successfully adapted for counting viable algae and protozoa.   Cultures of prey organisms may be used for the enumeration of known predators, and the method has already been used in combination with classical baiting techniques to obtain estimates of fungal propagules (Gaertner 1968).   With a little imagination it could provide at least semi-quantitative data where, at present, only qualitative information exists.   It should be possible, for example, to obtain an estimate of the number of infective fungal units in a water sample by inoculation into the appropriate algal host.   In particular, it should be possible to use media more closely resembling the natural environment.

5.3.3   *Analysis of Results*

Inoculum size, degree of replication and dilution ratio all affect the result obtained.   The effect of the first may be eliminated by adhering to a single size for all dilutions; this should be possible for all but the most dilute populations.

References to MPN tables for a range of dilutions and degrees of replication are given in Table 4.   The tables of Fisher & Yates (1948) are not actually MPN tables but are based on a slightly different estimate derived from the total number of positive and negative scores (Cochran 1950).   The precision of this estimate is equivalent to that of MPN tables and is, in fact, the one used by Harris & Sommers (1968) in their tables.

TABLE 4. SOURCES OF MOST PROBABLE NUMBER TABLES FOR DIFFERENT
EXPERIMENTAL DESIGNS

Dilution Ratio	Degree of Replication		
	5	8	10
10:1	Taylor (1962)[1]	Norman & Kempe (1960)[1] Harris & Sommers (1968)	Halvorson & Ziegler (1933)[1]
4:1	Fisher & Yates (1948)[2]	Harris & Sommers (1968)	Fisher & Yates (1948)[2]
2:1	Fisher & Yates (1948)[2]	Rowe et al. (1977)	Fisher & Yates (1948)[2]

[1] Copies of these tables are also published by Meynell & Meynell (1970).

[2] These tables of densities of organisms by the dilution method are also applicable to the other combinations of dilution ratios and degrees of replication.

The calculations and tables of MPN methods are based on the assumption that the microorganisms in the inocula are distributed in a random manner. A test for this assumption was devised by Moran (1954). This assumes that, at the extremes of the range of dilutions used, 100% positive and negative scores are obtained. The first step is to calculate the value of T from

$$T = \Sigma[n(N-n)]$$

where n is the number of positive scores at each dilution and N is the number of replicates. The observed value of T is compared with the expected value $E(T)$ (Table 6.3, Meynell & Meynell 1970) in calculating M from

$$M = \frac{T - E(T)}{S.E.(T)}$$

where $S.E.(T)$ is the standard error of T (Table 6.3, Meynell & Meynell 1970). If the results conform to a Poisson series then the probabilities of obtaining, by chance, values of $M \geqslant 1 \cdot 645$ or $\geqslant 2 \cdot 326$ are $\leqslant 0 \cdot 05$ and $\leqslant 0 \cdot 01$ respectively.

If a Poisson distribution is confirmed then the probability of Y organisms in an inoculum $[P_{(y)}]$ with a mean count m will be given by

$$P_{(y)} = e^{-m} \frac{m^y}{y!} \quad \dots\dots\dots(1)$$

where e is the base of natural logarithms.

The probability of a zero count in the inoculum will therefore be given by

$$P_{(o)} = e^{-m} \frac{m^o}{o!} = e^{-m} \dots(2)$$

and the probability of one organism being present (the theoretical minimum for growth) is given by

$$P_{(1)} = e^{-m} \frac{m^1}{1!} = e^{-m}.m \quad (3)$$

The greatest precision is obtained with an inoculum of 1·6 cells per tube (Meynell & Meynell 1970) and this is most likely to be achieved with a small dilution factor. This level corresponds to a score of 80% positive scores and since the probability of a zero score is given by equation (2) the probability of a positive score will be given by

$$P_{(+)} = 1 - e^{-m}$$

therefore

$$P_{(1.6)} = 1 - e^{-1·6} = 0·8, \quad \text{i.e. } 80\%$$

In practice however there is not much decrease in precision if the percentage of positive scores lies between 55% and 92%.

Apart from increasing the likelihood of obtaining this level of positive scores, the use of a low dilution factor produces narrower confidence limits. Thus the standard error, expressed as a percentage of the mean, is twice as large with a tenfold as with a twofold dilution factor.

Repeated estimates on a single sample often reveal a skewed distribution of the MPN about the mean, with a predominance of high values. The distribution of log MPN is however more symmetrical and it is recommended that standard errors and statistical tests be applied to this function (Bonde 1977; Cochran 1950).

The standard error of log MPN is given by

$$S.E. = 0·55 \sqrt{\frac{\log a}{n}}$$

where a is the dilution ratio and n the degree of replication. If $a = 10$, then 0·58 is used instead of 0·55, and the formula simplifies to

$$S.E. = \frac{0·58}{\sqrt{n}}$$

Confidence limits (95%) for log MPN are given by

$$\log \text{MPN} \pm 2.\text{S.E.}$$

Therefore the confidence limits for the MPN are obtained by *multiplying* and *dividing* the MPN by the antilog of the term 2.S.E.

Factors by which the MPN may be scaled to provide 95% confidence limits and standard errors are provided by Meynell & Meynell (1970), Harris & Sommers (1968) and Rowe et al. (1977).

To test for significant differences between two counts, t is calculated from

$$t = \frac{\log \text{MPN}_1 - \log \text{MPN}_2}{0 \cdot 55 \sqrt{\dfrac{\log a_1}{n_1} + \dfrac{\log a_2}{n_2}}}$$

where a is the dilution factor and n the degree of replication. Where $a = 10$ then $0 \cdot 55$ is replaced by $0 \cdot 58$. The value of t is compared with that of "Student's" t $(df = \infty)$. A simplified scaling system for comparison of the two MPN values is provided by Harris & Sommers (1968) for ten- and fourfold dilution series.

In addition to the above, when finally confronted with several dilutions the researcher must choose which sets of results to compare with the MPN table. The choice of dilution level is discussed in some detail by Meynell & Meynell (1970). The simplest procedures appear to be: (a) choosing the level where the middle dilution most closely approximates to the 80% positive scores; (b) if more than one set of dilutions exist between the extremes of 100% positive and 100% negative scores, then the geometric mean of their MPN is taken; (c) use of a method based on total number of positive and negative scores as in the table of Fisher & Yates (1948).

6. ESTIMATION OF BIOMASS

6.1 INTRODUCTION

There is usually no difficulty in measuring the biomass of a microorganism, as long as it is present in sufficiently large numbers and in pure culture.   These conditions are rarely met by the microbial ecologist, who is usually confronted with a more or less dilute suspension of a mixture of organisms, from which an estimate of the 'total' microbial biomass, or that of a particular group of organisms within the community, is required.   Biomass may be expressed in terms of wet weight, dry weight, cell volume, or a particular chemical component of the cell (e.g. carbon) per unit volume or weight of water or sediment, or per unit of total seston (particulate material) present.   For this reason the methods available for total seston are also summarized here.

6.2 ESTIMATION OF TOTAL SESTON

A known volume of sample is filtered and the material trapped on the filter is estimated.   The type of filter used will depend on the analysis to be performed.   It is first necessary to decide on the dividing line between 'particulate' and 'soluble' material.   The particles, living or non-living, found in natural aquatic samples represent a very wide range of sizes.   The presence of very fine colloidal material blurs the distinction between particulate and soluble matter.   It would be logical to use a filter which removed the smallest living particles (other than viruses) and to refer to the filtrate as the 'soluble' fraction.   In practice this means a filter with a pore size not greater than $0 \cdot 22 \ \mu$m.

Total seston may be determined as either dry weight or weight of carbon on the filter.   For dry weight determinations the filter is heated to constant weight at 80 °C, before and after filtration of the sample.   In both instances

the filter is cooled in a desiccator before weighing. This temperature (80 °C) is chosen to prevent loss of volatile oils from any diatoms which may be present. The results will obviously vary with the drying temperature used, and, if volatile components could create a serious error, it might be preferable to dry the samples under vacuum at room temperature, over a powerful desiccant such as phosphorus pentoxide.

Polycarbonate membranes are particularly suitable for such procedures because of their low uniform weight and their non-hygroscopic nature. Cellulosic membranes may also be used as long as care is taken to prevent adsorption of atmospheric moisture during the weighing process. Manufacturers also produce membranes specifically for gravimetric analysis (e.g. matched-weight pairs of the Millipore AA type or Gelman polyvinyl chloride membranes) but rarely are these available at $0.22\ \mu$m pore size.

If seston carbon is to be determined, a non-carbonaceous filter must be used. The only alternative is to use membrane filters and subtract 'blank' values for the filters. This will result not only in loss of sensitivity but also in an error term due to variability between filters. Glass-fibre filters are a suitable inert alternative, but must be preheated to 550 °C (usually overnight) to remove traces of carbon before use. Glass-fibre filters are not, however, graded into specific pore-size ranges although manufacturers will provide information on the minimum particle size removed and their performance characteristics have been determined by particle fractionation (Sheldon 1972). Thus Whatman GF/C filters have a nominal retention of $1.2\ \mu$m and GF/F filters of $0.7\ \mu$m. The latter are the equivalent of the Reeve Angel 984H glass-fibre filters, quoted by Wetzel & Otsuki (1974) as having a porosity of $0.3\ \mu$m to $0.5\ \mu$m when tested independently, and are similar to the Gelman type A/E filters. It is not possible, therefore, to obtain glass-fibre filters with the same low porosities as those of membrane filters. Tests at this laboratory on the effectiveness of glass-fibre filters in the removal of planktonic bacteria revealed that the GF/C and GF/F pads removed approximately 50% and 75% respectively, as determined by direct counts on the untreated samples and the filtrates. These results, of course, depend both on the proportion of smaller bacteria in the samples, and on the volume filtered.

After filtration, dry weight may be determined by heating at 80 °C as described above and loss on ignition by heating at 550 °C overnight. The particulate carbon content of the filters may be combusted and estimated by infra-red gas analysis, conductimetrically, in an automatic CHN analyzer, titrimetrically or spectrophotometrically after chemical oxidation (Strickland & Parsons 1968; Golterman, Clymo & Ohnstad 1978; Stainton et al. 1977; Mackereth et al. 1978). These methods may, of course, be applied to dried benthic material without prior filtration.

6.3 ESTIMATION OF TOTAL MICROBIAL BIOMASS

The methods given in this section are for estimation of the total biomass and not the fractions due to individual microbial groups. The ideal method will determine small quantities of the biomass indicator, which should be present in all living cells in a fairly constant proportion, and not found in the non-living components of the seston (detritus and dead cells).

6.3.1 *Adenosine triphosphate (ATP)*

This molecule, a carrier of the high-energy bonds essential to all vital processes, has become very popular as an indicator of biomass, largely because it is easy to assay and probably fulfills the above conditions better than most others.

The basis of the assay for ATP is its reaction with the luciferin – luciferase system of the firefly and the resulting emission of light according to the equation

$$\text{LUCIFERIN} + \text{ATP} + O_2 \xrightarrow[\text{Mg}^{++}]{\text{Luciferase}} \text{LUCIFERIN} + \text{AMP} + \text{P--P} + H_2O + hv$$
(reduced)   (oxidized)

Thus one photon of light is emitted for each molecule of ATP hydrolysed. An example of an application of the method to plankton samples is given by Holm-Hansen & Booth (1966), and discussion of more recent results by Holm-Hansen (1973), Karl & Holm-Hansen (1976) and Jones & Simon (1977).

The original method of Holm-Hansen & Booth (1966), which is also summarized by Vollenweider (1974), has been modified, in the light of recent developments, to improve the sensitivity and to reduce the interferences obtained with crude enzyme preparations.

The analytical method may be divided into the following steps.

a. Extraction of ATP from the sample

The extraction of ATP must be fast (no longer than a few tenths of a second) because of its extremely rapid turnover in the cell. The solution used for extraction could alter the factor used to calculate biomass C from ATP concentrations (see section *d*.). The proposed cellular carbon : ATP ratio of 250:1 (Holm-Hansen & Booth 1966) was obtained using Tris buffer extractions. Any alteration in the extraction procedure may affect this ratio and necessitate its recalculation using cultures and natural populations.

ATP from samples containing a large biomass of microorganisms (e.g. benthic material) may be extracted by direct injection, whereas it may be

necessary to concentrate some of the more dilute planktonic samples by membrane filtration before extraction.   Both methods have advantages and disadvantages.

In this laboratory the direct injection technique (Jones & Simon 1977) is used as follows: 1 ml of sample (water or a 5×10^{-3} dilution of sediment) is dispensed into 4 ml of actively boiling 0.02 M Tris or HEPES buffer (pH 7.8) held in a preweighed vial over a bunsen flame.   The vial, loosely capped, is then transferred to a medical steamer for 5 min, after which its external surface is dried and its weight brought up to vial weight $+5$ g with buffer.   If the contents are not to be analysed immediately, the vial cap is closed and the content are shaken before storage at -20 °C.   The buffer is filtered through a boiled 0.22-μm cellulosic membrane filter before use, and the vials are cleaned in boiling detergent solution (Decon 90), rinsed in double-distilled water and sterilized by dry heat at 170 °C for 1 h (or, preferably, fired at 550 °C overnight).   The vial caps are treated in the same manner except that the final heat treatment is at 100 °C.

When required, internal standards are added to samples in the volume ratio 1:5.   The internal standard is usually an enrichment of planktonic bacteria, produced by incubating lake water (previously filtered through a GF/C filter) overnight with a little added glucose and peptone.

Standard ATP solutions (10^{-3} M) are stored at -20 °C and diluted with 0.02 M buffer when required.   We have observed some apparent ATP loss from dilute ($<10^{-9}$ M) solutions and samples on freezing and thawing, and also during the boiling procedure, presumably due to adsorption on the glassware.   The results from stored samples should, therefore, be interpreted with care, and only after analysis of standards containing similar quantities of ATP which have been stored for the same period of time.   Similarly, standard solutions should be boiled in the same way as the test sample when constructing a calibration curve.

The internal standards are necessary to correct for extraction efficiency in the presence of planktonic or benthic material, and chemical interference. The latter can be considerable in organic sediments, hence the considerable dilution of the sediment before extraction.   Water samples from anoxic hypolimnia contain fewer organisms (the biomass is, on average, three orders of magnitude greater in the sediment) and chemical interference may cause quenching of the ATP light emission.   If this is not too severe the values may be corrected, using internal standards, but it is not uncommon for 100% quenching to occur.   Under these circumstances the membrane filtration technique must be used.

If plankton samples from oligotrophic waters or samples from anoxic hypolimnia are to be analysed, it may be necessary to filter them.   This concentrates the organisms from the former and reduces chemical

quenching in the latter. Whenever possible, hypolimnetic samples should be filtered under anaerobic conditions to reduce ferric iron precipitation on the membrane and possible stressing of obligate anaerobes. Cellulosic membranes, of $0.22 \mu m$ pore size, are used and these are rinsed in boiling extraction buffer before the sample is filtered, using the minimum of vacuum (650 Pa of vacuum $\approx$ 5 mm Hg or torr of vacuum). The membrane is removed, immersed immediately in 5 ml of actively-boiling extraction buffer, and then treated as described above for the direct injection method.

Membrane filtration may cause cell lysis and interference from detritus (Jones & Simon 1977) as well as a reduction in the adenylate energy charge (see *e*. below) of the cells (Karl & Holm-Hansen 1978). These effects may be reduced by using the minimum of reduced pressure but this is not always possible if it is necessary to filter large volumes of oligotrophic waters. A 'filtration effect' may also be observed (i.e. decreasing ATP yield per unit volume with increasing volume filtered) and therefore it is advisable to filter as small a volume as possible and to ensure that the ATP yield/volume response curve is linear at the volume used. Karl & Holm-Hansen (1978) attributed much of this 'filtration effect' to a reduction in adenylate energy charge; they observed no concomitant drop in total nucleotides (ATP+ADP+AMP).

b. Reconstitution of the luciferin–luciferase preparation

Firefly luciferase may be obtained in a purified crystalline form but as such is extremely expensive. Most laboratories use the crude enzyme extract, such as that obtained from Sigma Ltd, and the methods described here are suitable for such preparations.

The procedure used to reconstitute the enzyme preparation can have a marked effect on the sensitivity of the final mixture. There is also evidence that commercial preparations of the enzyme mixture are limited in luciferin, which when added to the mixture increases sensitivity. The following procedure has proved satisfactory when a low detection limit (*c*. 4 ng l^{-1} $\equiv$ 7×10^{-12}M) is required. The luciferin–luciferase enzyme preparation (50 mg FLE 50, Sigma Ltd) is dissolved in 7 ml of reconstitution mixture. This contains bovine serum albumin (0.1%), EDTA (1 mM) and $MgSO_4$ (10 mM), the pH of which is set to 7.4–7.6 with dilute KOH. The mixture is then stored overnight at 4 °C to extract (stirring during this period does not, apparently, improve the extraction efficiency). The mixture is centrifuged at 18 000 *g* for 10 min (at 4 °C) and the supernatant is then allowed to equilibrate for *c*. 1 h in the dark at room temperature. To 7 volumes of this supernatant are added 3 volumes of a 1 mg ml^{-1} D-luciferin solution (Calbiochem Ltd). The final concentrations of luciferin and enzyme preparation after mixture with the ATP sample are thus 100 μg ml^{-1}

and 1.67 mg ml^{-1} respectively. The D-luciferin is purchased as a powder but it is dissolved in buffer (pH 7.8) and dispensed into vials. All operations and the sealing of the vials are conducted under an atmosphere of nitrogen; the vials are then stored at -20 °C.

Enzyme reconstituted in this way is extremely sensitive but the addition of luciferin is very expensive, increasing the cost by 10 pence per assay. Karl & Holm-Hansen (1978) described a method in which the enzyme preparation was diluted to a greater degree, although the detection limit is increased to c. 500 ng l^{-1}. The luciferin–luciferase preparation (FLE 50, Sigma Ltd) is dissolved in 5 ml of distilled water and 10 ml each of 0.04 M MgSO$_4$ and 0.1 M KHAsO$_4$ buffer (pH 7.4). This is allowed to stand in the dark at room temperature for 4 h, centrifuged at 18 000 g for 10 min (at 4 °C), and is then ready for use.

c. Mixture of sample and enzyme preparation, and measurement of light emission

When the ATP sample and the enzyme preparation are mixed, a flash of light is emitted which has a peak of approximately 3 s duration, followed by a period of slower decay (Fig. 6).

The peak height of the light flash and the integral over the first 3 s are proportional to the ATP concentration. Longer periods of integration, or integration over the 15–75 s period as used by Holm-Hansen & Booth (1966), may lead to inaccuracies due to interference by other nucleotides, particularly GTP (see Fig. 6). These interferences are not as apparent when purified (crystalline) luciferase is used, but may be overcome with crude enzyme preparations either by peak height (or 3-s integral) measurements or by the addition of c. 800 ng ml^{-1} of guanosine diphosphate (GDP) to the luciferase preparation (Karl 1978). The dilution of the enzyme preparation as described above (Karl & Holm-Hansen 1978) ensures that non-ATP nucleotide-dependent light emissions are delayed, and the addition of GDP inhibits the formation of ATP from other nucleotides. The addition of GDP works satisfactorily with the more dilute enzyme preparation but higher blank values are obtained. The method is not satisfactory for use with the luciferin-enriched preparation because the values obtained for blanks and standards rise steadily with time.

In this laboratory satisfactory results have been obtained with an Aminco Chem-Glow photometer, although many suitable photometric instruments exist. The standard, or sample, is placed in the photometer in a disposable 50×6 mm tube and the luciferin–luciferase preparation injected through a septum. The optimum sample-to-enzyme-preparation ratio was found to be c. 2:1 and the volumes used are 266 μl and 133 μl dispensed from an adjustable microlitre pipette (Finnpipette) and a micro-litre syringe with a

repeating adaptor (SGE Ltd) respectively. For the most precise work the luciferase preparation is delivered from a constant-rate adjustable syringe. The peak height is measured, or a 3-s integral is obtained. Blank values, obtained by injecting the enzyme into extraction buffer, are

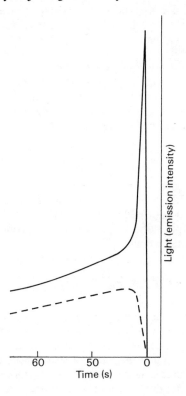

Fig. 6 Emission intensity light curve obtained when ATP (continuous line) and GTP (broken line) are mixed with firefly luciferin-luciferase.

subtracted. It is conventional to inject ATP samples into the enzyme preparation but there is no reason why the procedure should not be reversed. The method has the added advantage of a stable base line against which the light emission may be measured, and obviates the need for an electronic integrator which can cope with the negative signals produced

when buffer controls are injected into the luciferase preparation. Standard solutions of ATP are used with every test run, and the machine response is determined by linear regression. In the absence of added luciferin the response to ATP, particularly at low concentrations, is usually curvilinear, and calibration curves are often presented as double-log plots. When using the luciferin-enriched preparation described above, the response is usually linear for the range 5–800 ng l^{-1}.

d. Analysis of results and calculation of biomass.

The ATP concentration in the original sample may be calculated in one of three ways, using internal standards. The standard itself may be used as a single point calibration, and linearity of response with ATP concentration assumed. A factor (f) to correct for quenching and extraction efficiency is obtained from

$$f = \frac{EI_{is}}{EI_{s+is} - EI_s}$$

where EI_{is}, EI_{s+is} and EI_s are the emission intensities (light integral or peak heights) of the internal standard alone, the sample mixed with the internal standard, and the sample alone, respectively. The concentration of ATP in the sample $[ATP_s]$ is then calculated from

$$[ATP_s] = \frac{[ATP_{is}]}{EI_{is}} \cdot EI_s \cdot f$$

where $[ATP_{is}]$ is the ATP concentration in the internal standard.

More accurately, the ATP concentration equivalent to the corrected sample emission, $EI_s \cdot f$, may be obtained from a calibration curve. The response curve of the quench may also be used to obtain the sample ATP concentration, although this method requires many more analyses. Several internal standards of increasing concentration are added to aliquots of the sample, and the ATP concentration in the original sample is obtained from the negative intercept on abscissa in the regression of EI on added ATP concentration. This method should be the most accurate in that it allows for any change in quench with changing ATP concentration, although surprisingly good agreement was obtained when the three methods were compared using the enzyme preparation with added luciferin.

Data from early published work (Holm-Hansen & Booth 1966) indicated that the cellular carbon : ATP ratio was *c.* 250:1 for a wide variety of microbial cells, although this was known to range between 140:1 and 2000:1. More recently, results have shown that within a single algal species, in field conditions, the ratio may range between 200:1 and 5000:1

(Cavari 1976). The conclusion drawn was that the ratio of 250:1 may be a good indicator of bacterial biomass in hypolimnetic water, where algae and zooplankton are absent, and that ATP may be used as an indicator of nutrient limitation in phytoplankton. It is worth emphasizing that the original C : ATP ratio of 250:1 was obtained using a Tris buffer extraction. Any departure from this method may change the apparent ratio, and necessitate recalibration.

e. A note on total adenylates and adenylate energy charge

Karl & Holm-Hansen (1978) observed that the ATP concentration dropped with increasing volume of the sample filtered. Total adenylates (ATP+ADP+AMP), however, remained constant. Concentrations of ADP and AMP may be determined by enzymic conversion to ATP followed by analysis as outlined above. The method is essentially that of Chapman et al. (1971), although for details of its use in environmental samples it is advisable to consult Karl & Holm-Hansen (1978).

The adenylates are extracted as above and $900\,\mu l$ of the extract is incubated as follows:

1. For ATP: with $100\,\mu l$ of a solution containing
150 mM potassium phosphate buffer
pH 7·4
30 mM $MgCl_2$

2. For ATP+ADP: with $100\,\mu l$ of a solution containing
150 mM potassium phosphate buffer
pH 7·4
30 mM $MgCl_2$
1 mM phosphoenolpyruvate
320 International Units ml^{-1} pyruvate kinase

3. For ATP+ADP+AMP: with $100\,\mu l$ of a solution containing
150 mM potassium phosphate buffer
30 mM $MgCl_2$
1 mM phosphoenolpyruvate
320 International Units ml^{-1} pyruvate kinase
1250 International Units ml^{-1} myokinase.

The samples are incubated for 30 min at 30 °C and the reaction is stopped by boiling for 2 min. The boiling prevents cycling of adenylates during the luciferase reaction resulting in an atypical decay curve (Karl &

Holm-Hansen 1978). The only alternative is to use purified enzymes. ATP standards are incubated with each of the enzyme mixtures to determine and correct for the degree of quench for each treatment. Using the luciferin-enriched preparation of Jones & Simon (1977), it is possible to obtain reproducible results down to 10^{-8} M adenylates.

Incubation mixture 3 above provides a value for total adenylates and the adenylate energy charge (AEC) may be calculated as follows (Atkinson & Walton 1967)

$$AEC = \frac{[ATP]+0\cdot5[ADP]}{[ATP]+[ADP]+[AMP]}$$

The theoretical range for AEC is $0\cdot0$ to $1\cdot0$ although it has become generally accepted that growing cells have an AEC of $0\cdot8$ to $0\cdot9$. Environmental samples with an AEC of greater than $0\cdot7$ are considered to contain actively growing cells (Wiebe & Bancroft 1975; Karl & Holm-Hansen 1978) whereas those with values of less than $0\cdot6$ have tended to be thought of as less active. This latter interpretation should be considered carefully when dealing with mixed microbial communities, since some organisms have been shown to grow at maximum rates at AEC values of less than $0\cdot1$ (Edwards & Lloyd 1977). Further discussion on the interpretation of AEC values is provided by Knowles (1977).

6.3.2   *Deoxyribonucleic acid (DNA)*

Although DNA does not fulfil all the conditions of a biomass indicator, in that it may remain intact for some time after cell death, it may provide accessory information to that obtained from other determinations (e.g. Hobbie et al. 1972).

The method is, in essence, a procedure for the determination of the sugar deoxyribose and is based on the procedure of Kissane & Robins (1958), adapted for water samples by Holm-Hansen et al. (1968). A minimal volume of sample is filtered through a membrane filter using the minimum of reduced pressure, although Cattolico & Gibbs (1975) and Lien & Knutsen (1976) have obtained satisfactory results with cellulose and glass-fibre filters respectively. As with all filtration steps, the effect of the volume filtered on the response per unit volume should be checked before using the method routinely. Holm-Hansen et al. (1968) recommend the addition of diatomaceous earth to the membrane filter to aid extraction. The filter is then placed in a tube, 5 ml of acetone added, the mixture agitated and then allowed to stand for 20 min. After centrifugation at 1500 g for 5 min, the clear supernatant is carefully removed by suction. This extraction is

repeated with 3 ml aliquots of acetone until all the membrane filter material is removed. The remaining precipitate is then extracted with 3 ml 90% acetone, 5 ml 10% trichloracetic acid (TCA) at 5 °C, and twice with 5 ml 95% ethanol. For a discussion on the effect of various preliminary extraction procedures, see Herbert, Phipps & Strange (1971). One drop of a 0·5% solution of wetting agent is added to the remaining pellet which is then dried at 60 °C for 1 h, although better reproducibility may be obtained by drying at 20 °C (Cattolico & Gibbs, 1975). 0·1 ml of freshly-prepared 3,5– diamino–benzoic acid dihydrochloride reagent (DABA.2HCl) is added to cover the pellet at the bottom of the tube. This reagent is prepared by dissolving 0·4 g of DABA.2HCl (of the highest purity obtainable) in 1·0 ml of distilled water, immediately before use. Less pure forms of DABA should be treated with charcoal before use until clear or a pale straw colour. The pellet and the DABA.2HCl are not mixed but the tube is covered with parafilm and the whole placed in a shallow water-bath at 60 °C for 1 h. After 0·5 h of heating, the sample is mixed on a vortex mixer and replaced in the bath. When the heating period is complete, the tubes are removed and 5·0 ml of 0·6 M perchloric acid are added to each, and the contents are mixed and then centrifuged at 1500 g for 4 min. It is possible to optimize the fluorescence yield by careful control of the proportions of DNA and DABA. Setaro & Morley (1976), for example, obtained highest values by incubating up to 8 μg of DNA with 30 mg DABA.

If the samples are too concentrated, dilution in a solution of 0·1 ml of DABA.2HCl in 5·0 ml of 0·6 M perchloric acid is advised, although there is evidence to suggest that 1 M HCl used as the final diluent increases the stability of the fluorescent product (Cattolico & Gibbs 1976). DNA standards are prepared by dissolving highly polymerized DNA in 1 M NH$_4$OH.

The concentration of the DABA.2HCl–DNA complex is measured spectrofluorimetrically with an excitation maximum (λ_{ex}) at 420 nm and maximum emission (λ_{em}) measured at 520 nm.

Alternative fluorimetric procedures for DNA exist, including the determination of thymine by acetol fluorescence, or the reaction of DNA with cationic dyes such as ethidium bromide (Udenfriend 1962, 1969), but they appear to offer no significant increase in sensitivity over the DABA.2HCl method (linearity range 0·04 to 4 μg ml^{-1} of final extract). The method of Kapuscinski & Skoczylas (1977) appears to be 2 orders of magnitude more sensitive but has yet to be tested on natural samples. In this instance, as with the application to natural materials of all fluorescence analytical procedures, the researcher is strongly advised to check the efficiency of the extraction procedure and the possibility of reduction of fluorescence intensity by other materials in the sample. Such

quenching may be caused by humic materials, and is particularly marked in anoxic water samples (Jones & Simon, 1975b).

The careful use of internal standards should provide some quantitative data on the DNA concentrations in freshwater samples, but the problems associated with the technique and the absence of a universal carbon : DNA ratio for conversion to biomass terms suggest that the method is best used for comparative purposes only.

6.3.3 *Estimation of microbial biomass from cell volume*

Although it is possible to obtain an estimate of the biomass of each microbial group in a mixed population in this way, the final value may contain several error terms, including those in the following:

a. The estimated number of organisms and percentage viability
b. The estimated size of the organisms
c. The formula used to calculate the size of the organism
d. The conversion factor used from volume to dry weight or cell carbon.

In spite of these difficulties, the method may be the only one available under certain conditions, for example estimation of the biomass of certain benthic protozoa.

The first error term, that associated with the size and viability of the population, has been discussed in detail in chapters 3, 4 and 5. The size of individual organisms within a population will vary, and care should be taken in making measurements of cell width and length. If fixatives are to be used, then their effect on cell shape and size should be determined. The most reliable estimates will be obtained from fresh preparations, and if small cells such as bacteria are to be measured, then the use of phase-contrast microscopy is advised. This may also allow a more reliable differentiation of live and dead filamentous fungi than bright-field observation of stained preparations (Frankland 1975).

The biomass of filamentous algae, bacteria and fungi may be obtained from measurements of cell width and filament length. The latter may be estimated under the microscope or projected on a suitable screen for measurement. The measurement of smaller organisms may be hindered by the amount of light required to produce satisfactory illumination on the screen from high-power objectives. Alternatively, the filaments themselves are not measured, but the number of times they intersect a squared eyepiece graticule is used as a measure of their length. This method has been used satisfactorily for algae (Olson, 1950) and terrestrial fungi (Swift 1973b).

For organisms with a regular shape, first approximations of the cell volume may be obtained from formulae for known geometrical shapes (e.g. cylinder $\pi r^2 h$, sphere $4\pi r^3/3$, cone $\frac{1}{3}\pi r^2 h$). More complex volumes may be

determined by building solid scale models and measuring their displacement, or by using graphical/mathematical techniques (Michiels 1974). Alternatively, average volumes may be obtained from published tables such as those for algal species in Vollenweider (1974), and for ciliates in Michiels (1974), but these should not be used until the values have been checked against a few specimens from the site under investigation.

An alternative and more sophisticated method for biomass estimation involves the use of electronic particle-detection instruments such as the Coulter counter. A detailed description of such counters is beyond the scope of this small book, but a useful introduction is provided by Kubitschek (1969). More recent developments in instrumentation have allowed simultaneous estimates of the components of mixed populations, whose sizes have ranged from c. 1 μm^3 (bacteria) to 20 000 μm^3 (protozoa) (Drake & Tsuchiya 1973). It is for estimating protozoan biomass that the Coulter counter has found particular favour (Curds & Bazin 1977; Curds et al. 1978), largely because estimation of cell volume is almost the only method suitable for these organisms in mixed cultures. The disadvantages of the method are that it provides no information on the viability of the organisms, nor can it differentiate between cells and detritus. Used with care, however, it might provide useful information on plankton populations.

6.3.4 Conversion factors for biomass

Having obtained an estimate of the microbial biomass in terms of cell volume, the researcher might wish to convert this to units of dry weight or carbon. The most frequently-used factors appear to be

Dry weight = 20% of wet weight

and Cell organic carbon = 10% of wet weight*

although several others are discussed by Winberg et al. (1971). There appears to be less information about protozoa and fungi than about algae and bacteria, from which the above factors were derived. The wet weights are often derived from volume, assuming a cell specific gravity of c. 1. It should be emphasized at this point that the indiscriminate use of these or any other conversion factors may lead to serious errors (see for example, Banse (1977) for a discussion of some inherent problems with carbon : chlorophyll ratios). It is therefore advisable, wherever possible, to obtain this information from experimental or environmental material.

---

* If the algal population is largely composed of diatoms then cell organic carbon may be as low as 5% of the cell weight.

6.4 ESTIMATION OF BIOMASS OF SPECIFIC MICROBIAL GROUPS

The methods outlined in 6.3 provide no information on the contribution of individual microbial groups to the total biomass of microbes. If this information is required, the methods outlined below may be useful.

6.4.1 *Photosynthetic pigments*

The most abundant plant pigment is chlorophyll *a*, and it is often used to estimate algal biomass in planktonic and benthic communities. The assumption that there exists a constant relationship between biomass and chlorophyll content may not be justified (Banse 1977) but the method usually provides reasonable estimates, and is particularly useful for comparative work when the nature of the population does not change drastically. A value of 40 : 1 might be accepted as a guide to the ratio of carbon to chlorophyll *a* in algal cells but this, like all conversion factors, should be treated with extreme caution. A detailed discussion of the assumptions and problems of chlorophyll determinations is provided by Vollenweider (1974). The information given here will therefore be the minimum required to perform the analyses, with a brief discussion of the problems involved as seen in the light of more recent publications. It is advisable to bear in mind the function of these pigments and to prevent photo-decomposition by conducting as many of the handling operations as possible at low light intensities or in darkness.

6.4.1.1 *Algal chlorophyll*

Most determinations of phytoplankton chlorophyll have been made in hot methanol or cold acetone extracts. However, the chlorophyll of some algae, particularly benthic forms (small coccoid green and sheathed blue-green algae) may not be extracted completely with these solvents. It may be necessary, therefore, to turn to alternative solvents and harsher treatments (e.g. use of lysozyme, EDTA, sonication and freeze-thawing) to obtain efficient extraction. It would be unwise to assume that the procedures outlined below will work for every microbial community, and it is advisable to test the efficiency of the adopted procedure by repeated extraction, fluorimetry or fluorescence microscopy.

Of the two solvents commonly used, methanol would appear to be the more efficient and, although there is some evidence of a loss of chlorophyll *a* on boiling of the solvent (Holm-Hansen & Riemann 1978), other work (Heaney 1978) suggests that incomplete extraction occurs in cold solvent. The absorption characteristics in acetone of the various chlorophylls and

their degradation products are, however, better understood. Whereas some authors have chosen to extract in methanol and transfer to acetone for acidification (Marker 1972), others have acidified directly in methanol (Tett et al. 1975; Holm-Hansen & Riemann 1978). Clearly no single method will satisfy all conditions, and, although two procedures are outlined, the references cited should provide a guide to the recent literature on the subject.

a. Methanol extraction. A known volume of water is filtered gently through a membrane or glass-fibre filter; their relative porosities and the productivity of the water must be borne in mind. Benthic material may be extracted without prior concentration. The moist filter is removed and inserted in a test tube. A known volume of 100% methanol is added and the tube agitated. The methanol is sometimes saturated with H_2S to prevent oxidation and allomerization of the pigments (see references cited by Holm-Hansen & Riemann (1978)). The contents of the tube are then brought to the boil for a few seconds in a water bath, allowed to stand in the dark at room temperature for 10 minutes, and then cooled under the cold tap. The methanol is decanted (excess is squeezed from the filter) and then cleared by centrifugation or refiltration through a glass-fibre filter. The absorbance of the solution is determined at 665 nm and 750 nm, in a 4-cm cuvette if necessary. The absorbance at 750 nm is subtracted from that at 665 nm to correct for general turbidity and background absorption. The chlorophyll *a* concentration in the sample [Chl*a*] is given by the formula

$$[\text{Chl}a] \ (\mu g \ 1^{-1}) = \frac{V_e}{V_s} . \frac{f}{\ell} . A$$

where V_e is the total volume of the solvent extract in ml, V_s is the volume of the sample filtered in litres, ℓ is the light path in cm, A is the absorbance at 665 nm corrected for that at 750 nm, and f is a factor equivalent to the reciprocal of the specific absorption coefficient multiplied by 10^3. The specific absorption coefficient calculated by Talling & Driver (1963) of $71 \cdot 94 \ \ell \ g^{-1} \ cm^{-1}$ yields a value of $13 \cdot 9$ for f. Riemann (1978) has, more recently, calculated a specific absorption coefficient of $77 \cdot 9$, equivalent to a value of $12 \cdot 84$ for f. These appear to be the extremes in the range of f values currently used and it is obvious that this source of variability will be small in comparison with sampling errors, extraction efficiencies and factors used to convert chlorophyll concentration to biomass.

For the spectrophotometric determination of phaeopigments in methanol extracts, Holm-Hansen & Riemann (1978) recommend acidification with HCl to a final concentration of 3×10^{-3} M for 3 min, followed by neutralization (with 25 mg $MgCO_3$ ml^{-1} of extract) with stirring for 10 min.

b. Acetone extraction. The above procedure may be performed, with the following modification in the extraction procedure. The solvent, acetone at a final concentration of 90%, is added to the sample, which must be subjected to considerable agitation to ensure efficient extraction (e.g. ultrasonication or grinding in a tissue homogenizer). The extraction, which is less efficient than in methanol, proceeds in the cold and it is often necessary to leave the sample in the solvent overnight, preferably in a refrigerator. The advantage of this method is that more is known about the absorption characteristics of photosynthetic pigments in acetone, and it is possible to make correction for those other than chlorophyll *a*. This may be particularly important in benthic samples. The proportion of chlorophyll degradation products may also be determined as phaeophytin by acidification of the clarified extract.

A simple procedure for these determinations is as follows. The clarified acetone extract is placed in a cuvette and the absorbance measured at 665 nm and 750 nm. A volume of MHCl equivalent to 1/100 of the volume of the extract is then added to the cuvette and the contents are mixed carefully with a glass rod covered by plastic tubing. After 1 min the absorbances are re-read against acidified blanks. These values are not always stable, and are best read after a fixed period of acidification. The process of adding acid converts all chlorophyll *a* to its degradation product and therefore the true chlorophyll *a* concentration may be determined by difference from the formula

$$[\text{Chl}a]\ (\mu\text{g l}^{-1}) = \frac{V_e}{V_s} \cdot \frac{1}{\ell} \cdot [A - A_a] \cdot 2 \cdot 43 f$$

where A is the difference between absorbance values at 665 nm and 750 nm before acidification and A_a the difference after acidification. The value of $2 \cdot 43$, a correction factor derived from absorption coefficients of pure chlorophyll and phaeophytin, is extremely sensitive to spectrophotometer slit-width settings. The value for f is suggested variously as $11 \cdot 9$ (Wetzel & Westlake 1974) and $10 \cdot 48$ (Marker 1972). For further discussion of these factors, and those used to determine the relative contributions of chlorophylls *a, b* and *c*, the reader is referred to Vollenweider (1974) and Golterman, Clymo & Ohnstad (1978). The presence of bacterio-chlorophyll *c*, which absorbs at a similar wavelength (section 6.4.1.2), could cause interference, and prior separation by thin-layer chromotography may be necessary (Madigan & Brock 1976).

c. Chlorophyll fluorescence. This sensitive method is based on the excitation of chlorophyll with blue light at a wavelength of about 436 nm, and measurement of the emitted fluorescence at 685 nm. It may be used on